Vocationalism in Further and Higher Education

Vocationalism in Further and Higher Education presents a collection of research-based papers on the 'English model' of vocationalism and higher education. It argues that negative societal and political perceptions have hindered the debate about the significance and relevance of vocational education and training provision to learning, work and the economy. In this book, the writers offer unique solutions to the difficult questions that have emerged from their investigations into vocationalism in England.

This edited collection brings together a group of academic experts to report and discuss their findings from many years of evidence-based research on vocationalism at three levels: macro (national and policy making), meso (programmes and organization), and micro (individual learning and teaching). Chapters explore the key issues relating to the topic, such as policies, curriculum, learning and teaching and work contexts. The book reflects on the diversity of related programmes and discusses the applicability and relevance of the term 'vocationalism' in the light of current developments relating to higher vocational education, including occupation, employability and professionalism.

This book is a timely contribution to the debate on the 'English model' of vocational education and will be an essential resource for researchers, practitioners and postgraduate students in the fields of vocational education, technical and vocational education and training, work-based learning, politics and policy of education, teaching and learning, higher education and curriculum and pedagogy.

Sai Loo is an academic at the UCL Institute of Education, University College London.

Jill Jameson is Professor of Education, Chair of the Centre for Leadership and Enterprise, Faculty of Education and Health, University of Greenwich.

Vocationalism in Further and Higher Education
Policy, Programmes and Pedagogy

Edited by Sai Loo and Jill Jameson

LONDON AND NEW YORK

First published 2017
by Routledge
2 Park Square, Milton Park, Abingdon, Oxon OX14 4RN

and by Routledge
711 Third Avenue, New York, NY 10017

Routledge is an imprint of the Taylor & Francis Group, an informa business

© 2017 selection and editorial matter, Sai Loo and Jill Jameson; individual chapters, the contributors.

The right of the editors to be identified as the author of the editorial material, and of the authors for their individual chapters, has been asserted in accordance with sections 77 and 78 of the Copyright, Designs and Patents Act 1988.

All rights reserved. No part of this book may be reprinted or reproduced or utilised in any form or by any electronic, mechanical, or other means, now known or hereafter invented, including photocopying and recording, or in any information storage or retrieval system, without permission in writing from the publishers.

Trademark notice: Product or corporate names may be trademarks or registered trademarks, and are used only for identification and explanation without intent to infringe.

British Library Cataloguing in Publication Data
A catalogue record for this book is available from the British Library

Library of Congress Cataloguing-in-Publication Data
Names: Loo, Sai, editor. | Jameson, Jill, editor.
Title: Vocationalism in further and higher education : policy, programmes and pedagogy / edited by Sai Loo and Jill Jameson.
Description: New York, NY : Routledge, 2016.
Identifiers: LCCN 2016014919 | ISBN 9781138947047 (hardcover) | ISBN 9781315670331 (electronic)
Subjects: LCSH: Vocational education—England. | Occupational training—England. | Education, Higher—Aims and objectives—England.
Classification: LCC LC1047.G7 V64 2016 | DDC 374/.0130942—dc23
LC record available at https://lccn.loc.gov/2016014919

ISBN: 978-1-138-94704-7 (hbk)
ISBN: 978-1-315-67033-1 (ebk)

Typeset in Galliard
by Apex CoVantage, LLC

Printed and bound in Great Britain by
TJ International Ltd, Padstow, Cornwall

Contents

Lists of figures, maps, tables or cases   vii
Acknowledgements   viii
List of contributors   ix

1 Introduction: vocationalism in the English context   1
SAI LOO AND JILL JAMESON

SECTION 1
Policy   7

2 Still asking: a new direction for vocational learning or another *great training robbery*? Further research into and analysis of the contemporary reinvention of apprenticeships in relation to further and higher education   9
PATRICK AINLEY AND MARTIN ALLEN

3 Merger talk in further education: of whales and minnows, rhetoric and reality   22
GEOFFREY ELLIOTT

4 Groundhog Day again: making sense of a complicated mess: HIVE-PED research on FE student and apprentice progression to higher education in England   37
JILL JAMESON, HUGH JOSLIN AND SHARON SMITH

SECTION 2
Programmes   51

5 A question of identity: does it do what it says on the tin?   53
PRUE HUDDLESTON

6 Links between concepts of skill, concepts of occupation and the training system: a case study of Australia 65
ERICA SMITH

7 Training of FE teachers with occupational/vocational experiences: an approach using collaboration and evidence-based research 78
SAI LOO

SECTION 3
Pedagogy 91

8 "It's all about work": new times, post-Fordism and vocational pedagogy 93
JAMES AVIS

9 Constructions of knowledge through practice in general vocational education in England 106
ANN-MARIE BATHMAKER

10 Higher vocational learning and knowledgeable practice: the newly qualified practitioner at work 117
KAREN EVANS

11 Conclusion: global perspectives on vocationalism and the English model 131
JILL JAMESON AND SAI LOO

Index 141

Figures, maps, tables or cases

Figures

4.1	The post-compulsory education system in England	39
4.2	Advanced level apprenticeships progression in England 2006–07 to 2012–13	44
9.1	Instructions listed on the board for science practical task	111

Tables

5.1	Characteristics of 16–19 study programmes	56
6.1	State of Victoria. Funded enrolments and funding rates 2011 and 2013, selected courses ordered by proportion of female enrolments	70
7.1	Details of participants	81
9.1	General vocational qualifications in England 1970s–2010s	108
9.2	School and college research sites	110

Acknowledgements

The journey of this edited book started when the Convenors of the British Educational Research Association (BERA) Post-Compulsory and Lifelong Learning Special Interest Group, Bronwen Maxwell (then current), Sai Loo (current), Kevin Orr (outgoing) and Jonathan Tummons (current) coordinated a series of three events to commemorate BERA's fortieth anniversary in 2014. Experts in the field of vocational education and training were invited over the academic year 2014–15. These were held in three locations: UCL Institute of Education, University College London; the University of Birmingham; and the University of Durham. Six of these contributors have included chapters in this edited book. Jill Jameson, previously a Convenor of the BERA Post-Compulsory and Lifelong Learning Special Interest Group, is now a Convenor of the Educational Technology Special Interest Group and Principal Investigator for the ESRC Higher Vocational Education and Pedagogy (HIVE-PED) Research Seminar Series. She joined Sai Loo as a co-editor to support the writing and publication of the book, bringing in additional chapters from the HIVE-PED Seminar events.

In addition to the contributions of the Convenors and contributors, we were very lucky to have the full support of Nick Johnson, executive director of BERA in the publication of this book, and we thank Nick for his kind support.

We also thank the Economic and Social Research Council (ESRC) for funding for the Higher Vocational Education and Pedagogy (HIVE-PED) Research Seminar Series and the Department for Business, Innovation and Skills (BIS), which funded research presentations and findings that led to or are closely related to several chapters in this book.

We particularly acknowledge and thank all of the chapter authors and the participants in the various research projects on vocationalism reported herein, the reviewers, Denis Gleeson, Yvonne Hillier and Ian McNay for their support, as well as the editors of Routledge, Clare Ashworth and Thomas Storr, for bringing this book to fruition.

Contributors

Professor Patrick Ainley is Professor of Training and Education at the University of Greenwich School of Education and Training and a Visiting Fellow at New College, Oxford University. His books include *The Betrayal of a Generation: How education is failing young people*, Policy Press 2016; *Learning Policy, Towards the Certified Society*, Macmillan 1999; *Apprenticeship: Towards a New Paradigm of Learning* (edited with Helen Rainbird), Kogan Page 1999; *The Business of Learning, Staff and Student Experiences of Further Education in the 1990s* (with Bill Bailey), Cassell 1997; *Degrees of Difference, Higher Education in the 1990s*, Lawrence and Wishart 1994; *Class and Skill*, Cassell 1993; *Training for the Future: The rise and fall of the Manpower Services Commission* (with Mark Corney), Cassell 1990; *From School to YTS*, Open University Press 1988; with Martin Allen, *Education Make You Fick, Innit?*, Tufnell Press 2007; and *Lost Generation? New strategies for youth and education*, Continuum March 2010. You can find him on Facebook and/or follow him on Twitter as @Olloverkrumwall.

Dr Martin Allen has taught in secondary, post-16 and higher education. He was active in the National Union of Teachers for many years. His research on apprenticeships can be downloaded from www.radicaledbks.com. Patrick blogs with Martin Allen at http://radicaled.wordpress.com/, where their latest publications can be freely downloaded: *The Great Reversal, Young people, education and employment in a declining economy* (124 pages, ISBN 978-0-9575538-0-4) and *Education Beyond the Coalition, Reclaiming the Agenda* edited with Patrick Ainely (182 pp, ISBN 978-0-9575538-2-80). Also, *Another Great Training Robbery or a Real Alternative for Young People? Apprenticeships at the start of the 21st century*. ISBN 978-0-9575538-4-2, pp. 23.

Professor James Avis is Professor of Post-Compulsory Education and Training at the University of Huddersfield. His research interests lie in post-compulsory education and lifelong learning. He has written extensively on the policy contextualisation of further education, having addressed curriculum issues, methodological questions and teacher professionalism, as well as the lived experience of teachers and learners. He has a keen interest in the political economy of this sector and its policy contextualisation. His recent books include *Education, Policy and Social Justice: Learning and Skills* and *Teaching in Lifelong Learning*. His latest book is *Social Justice, Transformation and Knowledge*.

Professor Ann-Marie Bathmaker is Professor of Vocational and Higher Education at the University of Birmingham, UK. Her research focuses on questions of equity and inequalities in vocational, post-compulsory and higher education, particularly in relation to issues of social class. She has a particular interest in the role of further education colleges and their international equivalents in the provision of education and training. Her recent research includes a study of higher education and social class (the Paired Peers project), a study of the role and purposes of vocationally oriented University Technical Colleges for 14–19 year olds in England and research examining constructions of knowledge in general vocational qualifications.

Professor Geoffrey Elliott has taught in comprehensive schools, further, adult and higher education and has undertaken a range of leadership roles during his career. He is President of the Association for Research in Post-Compulsory Education and serves on the Board of the Office of the Independent Adjudicator for Higher Education. He edits the international peer-reviewed journal *Research in Post-Compulsory Education* and is currently Professor of Post-Compulsory Education at the University of Worcester, specialising in education policy, leadership and lifelong learning.

Professor Karen Evans is Professor at UCL Institute of Education, University College London. She is a leading researcher in the UK Economic and Social Research Council's Research Centre LLAKES, investigating Learning and Life Chances in Knowledge Economies and Societies. Her research interests are learning in life and work transitions, and learning in and through the workplace. She has directed major studies of learning and work in Britain and internationally, publishing widely in articles and books, including *Youth and Work Transitions in Changing Social Landscapes* (2013), *The Sage Handbook of Workplace Learning* (2011); *Improving Literacy at Work* (2011) and *Learning, Work and Social Responsibility* (2009).

Professor Prue Huddleston is Emeritus Professor and formerly Director of the Centre for Education and Industry at the University of Warwick. She has a particular interest in the 14–19 curriculum, focusing on vocational education and qualifications and work-related learning. Professor Huddleston has published widely on vocational learning and applied pedagogy. Before joining the University of Warwick, she worked within the FE sector, as a teacher and manager, also within community and outreach education. She has been involved in postgraduate teacher training for over 20 years. She is a member of the Education and Employer Engagement Taskforce Research Committee.

Professor Jill Jameson is Professor of Education, Chair of the Centre for Leadership and Enterprise, Faculty of Education and Health, University of Greenwich. Professor Jameson is Chair of the Society for Research into Higher Education and BERA Convenor for the Educational Technology (and previously Post-Compulsory and Lifelong Learning) Special Interest Groups. Jill is also Lead Guest Editor for the 2016 *British Journal of Educational Technology* Special Edition on Emerging Technologies and Authentic Learning in Higher Vocational Education. She was previously the Director of Lifelong Learning at Greenwich (2000–2004). Jill's books include *Researching Post-Compulsory Education* (2003, with Yvonne Hillier), *Leadership in Post-Compulsory Education* (2006), the *Ultimate FE Leadership and Management Handbook* (2007, with Ian McNay), and the *e-Learning Reader* (2012, with Sara de Freitas).

Hugh Joslin is an Educational Consultant and Project Manager at the University of Greenwich, specialising in research on the progression of vocational and other underrepresented students and social mobility. As part of the ESRC HIVE-PED team at the Centre for Leadership and Enterprise at Greenwich, Hugh, along with Professor Jill Jameson and Sharon Smith, has coauthored research reports analysing the progression to higher education of further education students from all colleges in England and has completed a series of studies looking at the progression patterns of apprentices. Hugh has also supported the ESRC Seminar Series' focus on higher vocational education and pedagogy. Prior to this research, Hugh was Director of a Lifelong Learning Network, following a career in adult guidance and further education.

Dr Sai Loo is an academic at UCL Institute of Education, University College London. Before joining the Institute, he taught accounting and finance at higher education institutions in undergraduate, postgraduate and professional programmes and in vocational areas in further education. Sai has worked in industry as a Chartered Accountant. His areas of interests are in the interdisciplinary approaches to defining, identifying and applying knowledge in settings relating to working, learning and teaching. He has published widely in international refereed journals, and some of these can be accessed at ioe.academia.edu/SaiLoo.

Professor Erica Smith holds a Personal Chair in Vocational Education and Training at Federation University Australia. She has published widely, mainly in the area of training policy, apprenticeships and traineeships, enterprise training, and vocational education and training (VET) practitioners. She has previously worked as a human resource manager and in community work, as well as in the VET sector, as a TAFE teacher and manager and as Director of a State Industry Training Advisory Board. Erica is co-chair of INAP, the International Network on Innovative Apprenticeship. She has been invited to advise the Australian and overseas governments, as well as a range of NGOs. Erica also convenes the Australian Council of Deans of Education Vocational Education Group, representing those universities providing VET teacher education.

xii *Contributors*

Sharon Smith, Consultant Researcher for the University of Greenwich BIS Progression Tracking Research Project and ESRC HIVE-PED Seminar Series at the Centre for Leadership and Enterprise, working alongside Hugh Joslin and Professor Jill Jameson. Sharon is an expert research data analyst with more than 12 years' experience working on widening participation research. Previously Research and Evaluation Manager for the University of Kent (2003–13), Sharon is a member of the HEFCE Aimhigher Evidence Steering Group, Chair of the National Aimhigher Data Network, Chair of the South East Aimhigher partnership data group (MoRE) and an Action on Access WP Data Associate. Sharon leads the Kent & Medway Progression Federation Higher Education Access Tracker (HEAT), a national project involving longitudinal tracking of students across the student life cycle.

1 Introduction
Vocationalism in the English context

Sai Loo and Jill Jameson

One of the characteristics of the post-compulsory education sector in England and in a range of other countries such as Scotland, Australia and New Zealand is the teaching of programmes with a vocational route to work. In England, however, this general picture is also complicated by the fact that there is also a growing trend in secondary schools of providing such vocation-related courses. This is the result of the efforts of previous and current UK governments to 'open-up' educational opportunities (in terms of the types of teaching institutions and curricula) to learners. There is also a perception, deriving from centuries of social stratification and selectivity in the status and provision of different kinds of education in England, that vocational education is inevitably more narrowly utilitarian, less influential and less important than its more academic cousin: advanced ('A') levels. This divide between the sectors of 'vocational' and 'higher' education, in many ways peculiarly English, is also reflected in higher education institutions and in occupations (in terms of academic credentials and a number of related provisions). These academic-vocational divisions in the 'English model', together with negative societal and political perceptions, have to some extent stymied the debate regarding the significance and relevance of vocational education provision to learning, work and the economy. Should we, and, if so, can we, move past these ancient divisions, bounded by historical ties and allegiances, into a new understanding of what 'vocationalism' can mean in the twenty-first century? We open up the debate on the 'English model' of vocationalism with a recognition, first, of the complexity of the field and, second, with an understanding that there is a need to examine the research evidence within it before considering pathways to the future for an improved understanding and offering of 'vocational' provision.

This edited book on the vocationalism in higher (HE) and further education (FE) therefore aims to bring together into a 'Reader' a selection of academic experts to report and discuss their findings from many years of evidence-based research on vocationalism at three levels in England – macro (national and policy making), meso (programme and organization) and micro (individual learning and teaching). The book aims to debate some of the main issues relating to vocationalism in higher and further education, such as the policies, curriculum, learning and teaching and work contexts in which this term occurs. Our authors reflect on the diversity of vocationally related programmes and discuss the applicability and relevance of the conventional term 'vocationalism' in the light of current developments relating to higher vocationalism, such as higher vocational education, occupation, employability and professionalism.

We were convinced that there is a need for such a book, as there is still a lacuna of publications on this topic. In discussions with colleagues in the BERA Post-Compulsory Education and Lifelong Learning and the Educational Technology Special Interest Groups there was general agreement that a book of this kind was to be welcomed to update educational researchers and practitioners in the field. We also received support from colleagues in the ESRC Higher Vocational Education and Pedagogy (HIVE-PED) Research Seminar Series and its many partner institutions, and we have linked various sections in the book to presentations at Research Seminar events organised both by the BERA Special Interest Groups and to the ESRC HIVE-PED Series.

This book therefore aims to offer, from prominent researchers in the field, a collected volume of research-based papers on vocationalism and higher education that particularly focus on the 'English' model. While there is no one 'answer' to the difficult questions that have emerged in our investigations on vocationalism in England, the experts we have gathered together provide a series of refinements to the troubling questions that have hitherto shaped the field and, in some cases, they offer unique solutions that have emerged as a result of their work.

Part 1: Macro perspectives: National and policy making

In part 1, the first of three chapters on policy, contributed by Patrick Ainley and Martin Allen, provides a present-day analysis of higher-level apprenticeships (equivalent to first degree level) in England. Chapter 2 therefore provides an overview of policy developments on apprenticeships during the last four decades in England and their repeated failures to "replace industrial apprenticeships" (p.) since the collapse of these opportunities in the 1970s. The authors explain this in terms of policy makers' 'inability to re-build the vocational route'. This is due, in part, to the decline of the manufacturing sector relative to the service industry and also, in part, because of the continuing social divisions between provisions for traditional manual trades offered by FE institutions and that for non-manual professions provided by higher education institutions (HEIs). Ainley and Allen cite evidence of the low take-up of higher-level apprenticeships, which they view as a possible alternative to the university route. They lament the lost opportunity that had previously resulted from combining the pedagogical principles offered by further education (education 'with practice') and higher education (education 'with theory') or "thick HE" (p.). Drawing from empirical evidence, the authors view this attempt of higher-level apprenticeship offerings as yet another failure, along with the recurring mistakes made across the past four decades, to provide learners with an alternative to the traditional university route. Ainley and Allen examine the precariousness of the FE sector in the provision of vocational training. The sector has been challenged on two fronts simultaneously, as private training providers have entered the marketised sector and post-1992 HEIs have increased their offer of provision in vocational areas, such as engineering, that traditionally were offered by FE.

In Chapter 3, Geoffrey Elliott investigates leadership in FE institutions in this neo-liberal era. Drawing on empirical data from 11 FE and sixth-form college principals, he identifies five themes of metaphors (especially "the market in education" (p. 31) with positive and negative connotations by the interviewees): sustainability (significantly in terms of the size and financial aspects of the teaching institutions), quality (and the link with Ofsted [Office for Standards in Education, Children's Services and Skills] and funding), community (in terms of the local community in which the institutions are located and its possible counter to business considerations), policy (with its links to the positive and negative elements of market forces) and control (as expressed by the principals' ambitions and desires). Elliott (p.) concludes that mergers in the sector are "a clear consequence of the introduction of a real market in further education and as a vivid expression of business interests prevailing to the cost of educational ones". Elliot warns of the "high cost of reduced community engagement, fewer educational opportunities and severing of formerly collaborative partnership arrangements".

Chapter 4 by Jill Jameson, Hugh Joslin and Sharon Smith applies a 'Groundhog Day' metaphor to the post-compulsory education sector to summarise the entrapment of continuously repeating cycles of dysfunctionalities in which the overbureaucratisation of FE-HE apprenticeship qualifications, Management Information Systems (MIS) and funding systems has densely obscured understanding and obstructed learner progression pathways. Those in the sector struggling with apparently endlessly repeating winter days of austerity are keen to find solutions that enable the system to work. The University of Greenwich ESRC HIVE-PED (Higher Vocational Education and Pedagogy) Research Seminars team complemented their work in the Seminars with a Department of Business, Innovation and Skills (BIS) funded longitudinal investigation into the progression of learners from FE and apprenticeships provisions into HE. The team linked learner data from Individual Learner Records (ILR) and HESA, working with support from HESA, matching ILR records with HESA datasets, to identify and analyse data on college students and apprentices progressing to HE in FE and to HE. To break through the impenetrable impasse separating the complex ILR and HESA systems, they sought to understand progression rates, achievements and trends of specific learner cohorts by mode and course into non-prescribed and prescribed HE over time, analysing these against demographic and regional data. The resulting patterns were then mapped against the existing literature on progression, using a sense-making framework (Weick, 2012). This paper provides ground-breaking progression data, demonstrating how this might be utilised to provide benefits for learners and providers.

Part 2: Meso perspectives

The next three chapters relate to VET programmes at the 'meso' level of analysis. In Chapter 5, Prue Huddleston discusses the challenges of designing and delivering 'strong and credible' vocational courses for +14 learners. She provides a historical perspective of vocational programmes in England and laments the lack of understanding of 'vocationalism' by policy makers. Huddleston offers two factors to explain this confusion: 1) the inclusion of non-academic subjects as 'vocational' and 2) the negative perceptions of vocational education and the low quality of its programmes to date. She argues for an integrated approach to offering successful vocational courses. This includes guiding young learners to achieve an appreciation of the work-related nature of VET programmes, staffing teachers with the relevant occupational experiences, having access to real learning environments with 'industry-standard facilities and equipment' and offering effective and independent advice and guidance.

In Chapter 6, offsetting the 'English model' against that of other countries such as Australia, Erica Smith offers an investigation based on empirical data from two projects in which she discusses the concepts of skill, occupation and the training system in Australia. In the Australian vocational education and training system, she distinguishes apprenticeships and traineeships in relation to government policies. Drawing on interviews and focus groups with relevant stakeholders such as employers and training providers, Smith provides evidence for a clear connection between the perceived 'low-skilled' occupations such as in retail, hospitality, cleaning and security services and the reduction in funding, with a particular negative impact on female employment. This policy results in a reduction in traineeship numbers despite findings of a nuanced understanding of skills in all occupations. These findings are in contrast to the perceived 'skilled' jobs associated with apprenticeships where the funding has not been as adversely affected. Smith is critical of the social constructions of 'low-skilled' occupations associated with traineeships and the 'higher-skilled' occupations of apprenticeships in Australia, which have exacerbated the division between the two forms of training, resulting in an unfortunate gender impact.

Carrying on with the 'meso level' theme on occupational training, Chapter 7 focuses on the education of teachers with occupational experiences who teach on occupation-related/vocational programmes in the further education sector in England. The backdrop to this chapter relates to the voluntary nature of teachers obtaining a teacher training qualification. Besides being critical of the abandonment of compulsory teacher training in FE, Sai Loo provides two lines of argument: 1) the importance of teacher knowledge in a teacher education curriculum and 2) a pedagogical solution to training them. He uses Bernstein's concepts of knowledge and recontextualisation and Young's 'powerful knowledge' to critique teacher knowledge and reflective peer review and multimodality concepts to investigate a '360 degree' teacher training approach to enhancing teaching. Loo uses empirical data from two projects to discuss the two arguments and adds to the debate of including teachers' occupational experiences in teaching knowledge in the sector.

Part 3: Micro perspectives

The third part of this book reflects the investigations into the pedagogies of vocationalism, starting with Chapter 8 by James Avis, who conceptualises vocationalism from the standpoint of England as a knowledge-based economy. He theorises a form of vocational pedagogy in which its role is to develop "a creative and innovative workforce" (p.). Using the 'New Times' construction as a starting platform, he argues that it can offer transformative possibilities for the workforce in a post-Fordist economy in which creativity is seen as significant, workers contribute to the success of the organisations they work for and development of a collective intelligence offers opportunities in more egalitarian and democratic relations between workers and businesses. However, Avis is critical of the English model involving an Anglo-Saxon construction of vocational pedagogy, which is geared towards the world of work only, unlike other societies which offer wider forms of learning that include civic and academic education. Avis suggests that vocational pedagogy from a post-Fordist approach should offer more than just disciplinary knowledge, which may be applied to work settings and also include a social justice agenda, i.e. a social construction of knowledge. Johnson (Education Group, 1981: 37) has identified this as "really useful knowledge", gained in order that learners are able to "evaluate and judge the claims made by academic disciplines" (p.).

In Chapter 9, Ann-Marie Bathmaker considers constructions of knowledge as they take shape through practice in general vocational education in England. Based on the Knowledge in Vocational Education project, a 2010–11 Edexcel-funded, one-year research study, the chapter considers how pedagogic recontextualisations of knowledge occur in everyday practice, determined not only by available resources but also by students' needs. Confusions around the nature and the role of knowledge were evident from earlier research. The project investigated definitions and practice-based translations of the 'knowledge' provided in general vocational education qualifications in England and the ways in which teachers construct and translate knowledge within everyday pedagogic practices. Solutions to the problematic translation of theoretical, applied and work-related knowledge for middle- and low-achieving students are necessary to ensure continuing quality in general vocational education.

This final contribution from Karen Evans in Chapter 10 offers an empirically focused concept of 'Putting Knowledge to Work' in which different forms of knowledge such as "disciplinary, work-based and practice-based" (p.) are used to investigate how learning by those in different settings such as work and learning institutions utilise their know-how (knowledge and experiences). She uses data from higher vocational and professional areas of aircraft maintenance engineering, nursing and film and TV to investigate how knowledge may be applied in the different contexts. This conceptual framework consisting of four types of recontextualisation, represents a development of this process from those by Bernstein, Barnett and van Oers. Evans offers an alternative approach to 'transference' in understanding how learners acquire the types of knowledge that are necessary for eventual work applications and in so doing develops the "debate beyond the 'joining' of different knowledge forms (Billett, 2009) to focus attention on underlying social processes" (p.).

In the 'Conclusion', the editors consider again the focus of 'vocationalism' in the context of the continuing divide between higher and further education and the generally low status and reductions in funding for the VET sector in the 'English model'. The editors call for a reconsideration of the divisions between the higher and further education sectors in England with respect to 'vocationalism' and the opening up of new pathways for greater parity, progression and enhanced social mobility in vocational education across the entirety of England's educational provision.

References

Billett, S. (2009) Realising the educational worth of integrating work experiences in higher education. *Studies in Higher Education*, 34(7), 827–843.

Education Group CCCS (1981) *Unpopular Education*. London, Hutchinson.

Weick, K. E. (2012) Organized sensemaking: A commentary on processes of interpretive work. *Human Relations*, 65(1), 141–153.

Section 1
Policy

2 Still asking

A new direction for vocational learning or another *great training robbery?* Further research into and analysis of the contemporary reinvention of apprenticeships in relation to further and higher education

Patrick Ainley and Martin Allen

Introduction

Much water has flowed under the bridge since we first asked at an ESRC HIVE-Ped seminar in February 2014 whether the reinvention of apprenticeships by the Coalition government represented a new direction for vocational learning in the UK or was merely another great training robbery (Allen & Ainley, 2014). Notably there was the unexpected general election result in May 2015 so that the outcome which we and many others anticipated – namely, a 'two nation' approach from what Avis called 'one nation labour' (2014), dividing all school, college or training participants into either students or apprentices at 18, is now being implemented by a Conservative rather than a Labour government. Indeed, after the election, the Conservative government unexpectedly announced a return to a training levy on large employers to finance their promised 'three million apprenticeships' – a proposal that Labour had rejected as an electoral commitment to fund their promise of as many apprentices as students. Although the levy annoyed employers' organisations such as the Confederation of British Industry (CBI), it answered the question of where the funding for the three million was to come from. The new government has also scrapped maintenance grants for undergraduates, replacing them with loans which will fall most heavily upon poorer students. This may drive some would-be university applicants to consider apprenticeships instead, while partial economic recovery affords the possibility of direct entry to employment for others (see the following section).

However, our previous scepticism about the contemporary reinvention of apprenticeships was based not only on the record of repeated failure to replace industrial apprenticeships after they collapsed in the 1970s – first by a series of youth training schemes in the 1980s, then by John Major's Modern Apprenticeships in the 1990s ('modern' because 'flexible' and no longer fixed time served), followed by New Labour's Welfare to Work and subsequent Train to Gain in the new century – but also on what we took to be the reason for this inability to 'rebuild the vocational route'. Owing to the development of modern production, most employers do not really want or need apprentices – as seen from the CBI mentioned earlier. They wanted them for free perhaps but not enough to pay for them! The economic downturn has accelerated longer-term structural changes, particularly the collapse of many of the manufacturing trades with which apprenticeships have been associated, while large sections of production have also been downsized, outsourced and automated so as to require far fewer employees, even as productivity increases. As a result, the UK's post-industrial economy is largely based upon increasingly deregulated services employing semi-skilled, insecure and fungible labour. The continued decline of manufacturing means that most apprenticeships are in the following sectors, in this order: business; administration and law; health, public services and care; retail and commercial. These typically generate low-grade, badly paid, insecure jobs predominantly undertaken by women, which explains why women make up 50 per cent of intermediate level apprentices. (Since they also make up the majority of students, this adds to the mystery of the disappearing boys who are presumably going instead into unskilled work but since there is no longer a coherent Careers Service, there is no way to tell.)

As digitisation gathers pace in what Brynjolfsson and McAfee (2014) call the 'second machine age', vocational preparation from earlier and earlier ages for occupations that may no longer exist by the time training for them is complete seems singularly inappropriate. So too does cramming for academic qualifications that function as proxies for more or less expensively acquired cultural capital to gain entry to the hierarchy of higher education institutions. Rather, the education of a general intellect would surely be a more adequate preparation for

> fully developed individuals, fit for a variety of labours, ready to face any change of production, and to whom the different social functions they perform, are but so many modes of giving free scope to their own natural and acquired powers.
>
> (Marx, 1971: 494)

In addition, since 1981, when the Thatcher government repudiated the 1944 Employment Act's commitment to maintain full employment, post-war full employment and limited upward social mobility have never been restored despite reiterated promises by successive governments. Instead, in conditions of general downward social mobility in the new century (Roberts, 2010), a reserve army of labour has been reconstituted permanently "cycling between low-paid work and unemployment" (Clark & Heath, 2014: 258, n.60). The numbers structurally unemployed at any one time ratchet up with every crisis (Gamble, 2009), but in the 1980s, they bottomed out at around two million, though more recently this is complicated by aggressive welfare policing driving many off the claimant count and into part-time work (Lansley & Mack, 2015), as well as by the disproportionate representation of young people in this marginal status, whether in or out of nominal education or training. However, contrary to the impression given in the popular press, very few of this so-called 'underclass' are the same people plunged permanently into a 'culture of poverty'; rather, as Shildrick *et al.* (2010) found in Glasgow and Teeside, most churn through part-time, insecure and low-paid jobs intermitted by periods of unemployment.

This then is the context in and for which the latest 'apprenticeships' have been reinvented as an all-purpose panacea and it does not seem to us an auspicious one.

Apprenticeships under the coalition

It can be argued that education and training (learning) policy (Ainley, 1999) played a large part in reinforcing the new divisions of knowledge and labour outlined earlier. In her 2011 *Review of Vocational Education* for the Coalition, Alison Wolf argued that UK vocational awards (level 1 and 2 in particular) provided low or even negative labour market returns and that 350,000 young people – between a quarter and a third of the post-16 cohort – got "little or no benefit" (p.7) from post-16 education. With figures showing the number of key stage 4 vocational 'equivalents' achieved approaching 500,000, Wolf suggested that vocational learning should only make a 'limited contribution' and comprise no more than 20 per cent of a young person's curriculum offer and that apprenticeships would provide much higher rates of return to many young people by giving them workplace experience. She recommended that employers be paid to take on 16–18 year olds, providing that apprentices also received clearly defined off-the-job training and education.

Accordingly, from October 2012, apprentice frameworks had to include functional skills certification in numeracy, literacy and Information and Communications Technology (ICT) if considered relevant to the jobs the framework applies to – though apprentices who have achieved a C grade at GCSE are exempt from functional skills tests. There was also supposed to be coverage of personal learning and thinking skills that had been added to the schools' curriculum. This could be difficult since apprenticeships are designed to be delivered in the workplace. Department for Business, Innovation and Skills (DBIS) is clamping down on 'programme apprenticeships' where young people were based with training organisations to complete their work placements. Smaller employers, less able to provide the necessary training 'in-house', relied on the growing number of private training providers, who sidelined the FE colleges. After some serious concerns about quality and standards, training providers became subject to regular monitoring and inspection through Ofsted. Because training organisations claimed back much of the cost of training apprentices from the central government, they played an active role in the recruitment of employers. According to the 2012 *Richard Review of Apprenticeships* (Richard, 2012: background evidence, p.11), 27 per cent of employers said that the main reason for taking on an apprentice was because of an approach from a training organisation, compared to only 12 per cent who identified a skills need. The *Review* was produced by *Dragons' Den* entrepreneur Doug Richard and commissioned by the Coalition to examine apprenticeships as a result of concerns about quality and also the Skills Funding

Agency's (SFA's) record that more than one in three starting apprenticeships in 2011–12 were over 25. The *Review* recommended a move back to traditional models of apprenticeship targeted at those "who are new to a job or role that requires sustained and substantial training" (Richard, 2012: 18) so that already employed, older staff could not be subsidised by being counted as 'apprentices' as had happened in some notorious cases, e.g. ASDA as reported in the *Telegraph* (28/10/11). SFA data shows over a quarter of apprenticeships now being started by those under 19 years old.

The 2011 Education Act had created a duty on government to make 'reasonable' efforts to ensure employers provide apprenticeship training and the National Apprenticeship Service (NAS) published a *Statement on Apprenticeship Quality* in May 2012 outlining minimum standards. According to the House of Commons library apprenticeship statistics (Delebarre, 2015), expected costs had reached £1.55 billion by 2012–13 when they constituted almost a third of the entire adult skills budget, itself cut by 40 per cent under the Coalition. In a return to the pre-modern model, the NAS stipulated that all apprenticeships should be for at least 12 months and all apprentices should spend at least 280 hours a year in 'guided learning' and 100 hours or 30 per cent (whichever is greater) of all guided learning must be delivered 'off-the-job'. The DBIS's own survey put average apprentice wages at just over £6 per hour, with only 71 per cent receiving the minimum amount they should get based on their year and/or age (DBIS, 2013b). (From October 2015 the National Minimum Wage was £6.70 per hour, while the National Living Wage of £7.20 per hour plus eligibility to housing benefits marks the new age of majority at 25.)

Although all apprenticeships are supposed to provide technical knowledge and some general education, National Vocational Qualifications (NVQs) are still central to assessment. NVQs are based on a 'behaviourist' model of competence-based training (Hyland, 1994) with learners reduced to passive performers of prescribed tasks rather than being active agents. The NVQ preoccupation with learning 'outcomes' ignores how learning takes place and for Brockmann *et al.* (2008), the NVQ marginalises theoretical knowledge, while for Smithers (1997), it has destroyed the established and respected technical education of the post-war years. However, new qualifications are now promised!

Richard's headline recommendation to put 'employers in the driving seat' was regarded as 'risky' by Chris Jones, chief executive of the City & Guilds Group, reported in *FE News* (05/12/13):

> It's the assumption that employers have the time – and indeed the will – to cope with the additional bureaucracy these reforms will entail . . . Rather than incentivising employers, I fear they'll be put off by what's been announced.

Indeed, Martin Allen's prediction on the *Guardian*'s Further Education leadership and management website (10/07/14) that it would lead to a reduction in apprentice numbers may be born out subsequently. The Institute for Public Policy Research's most recent survey with local authorities confirms "a mismatch of supply and demand" with "1.8 million applications for 166,000 vacancies (a ratio of eleven applications for each vacancy)" (Raikes, 2015: 23). So that "There appears to be a mismatch between the apprenticeships people want to take on and the vacancies available." (p. 4) Raikes also lists other 'major concerns':

> Two-thirds of apprentices (67 per cent) at level 2 or level 3 are people who were already employed by their company, rather than new recruits.
> Since 2010, 42 per cent of starting apprentices have been over the age of 25, rather than being young people finding their way into work.
> A significant proportion of companies are failing to comply with the apprenticeship minimum wage, particularly in sectors such as hairdressing and children's care, and to the particular disadvantage of young people.
> (Raikes, 2015: 23).

Meanwhile, private training organisations – rather than FE colleges – have been the major financial beneficiaries in a climate where, as with education in general, government chased its own targets. This was one of the lacerating criticisms made by Wolf in a report published immediately after the election in June 2015:

> It is hard to find a single central government budget, and impossible to find another part of the education budget, that has been subject, in this period, to as much deliberate reordering and as many centrally directed changes in exactly how money is spent.
> (Wolf, 2015: 88)

She suggests this is because FE lacks the electoral influence with government and media of schools and HE:

> Consequently it is easy for ministers to initiate major changes in "skills" through a combination of principled and career reasons.
> (Wolf, 2015: 88)

Also because

> a "skills-based" approach . . . involved a number of underpinning beliefs which were very strongly held by both key ministers and key officials in Her Majesty's Treasury (HMT) and BIS, dating back to the late 1980s . . . derived from a fairly simple view of human capital theory.
> (p.19)

This led to the competence-based, behavioural approach to training noted earlier with funding paid for 'outcomes' achieved in "an interlocking set of incentives which drove down quality" (p.39).

The financial incentives associated with "payment by results" and a government drive for numbers' not only "help to explain why there has been a regular series of scandals and cases of fraud involving non-college private providers" (p. 27) but also why the

> system . . . is not producing highly qualified technicians at a time when there is strong labour market demand for them and when many of those currently in work are nearing retirement. Similar patterns are evident for key craft occupations (where gaps have been filled, at least temporarily, by immigration) and for mid-level health professionals. Apprenticeship numbers are overwhelmingly in areas which are cheap to deliver. Among apprenticeships which lead to a higher-level craft or technician level award (level 3 or above) less than five per cent are in engineering, manufacturing technologies or science.
>
> (p.39)

Familiarly, there are

> high levels of unemployment among the young, especially the less educated. A promised "rebalancing" of the economy towards more manufacturing has not materialised, but there is a large trade deficit. There are more graduates than ever before, and yet employers, notably in engineering, are nonetheless complaining about acute skills shortages.
>
> (p.2)

Heading for the precipice deals with the two sectors (as we still think of them in the UK but not in the USA – see Harbour, 2015) of FE and HE together, which is our own approach in this chapter and essential to any consideration of possibilities for higher vocational pedagogy. Wolf (2015) asks, *Can further and higher education funding policies be sustained?* (our emphasis), pointing out that 'Resources for teaching in the adult skills [FE and 'other providers'] area have declined; resources for teaching in universities have increased; and the gap between the two is large and widening' (p.4). Wolf considers this not only 'unsustainable' but 'deeply inegalitarian' and 'inefficient' (p.76).

Aiming higher or going further?

This is a problem some in government wish would just go away – as Hodgson and Spours recount: 'Vince Cable's revelation that DBIS officials proposed FE colleges be abolished to save money and no one would notice' (in Hodgson, 2015: 204). It cannot easily be achieved, however, despite the current 'area reviews' being undertaken by DBIS, with perhaps five million full and part-time FE students, depending how you count them. It is nevertheless a view shared by many academics, who just wish to be left alone to continue their familiar activities, like so many cartoon characters who have run off the edge of a cliff but, because they have not noticed, keep on running in mid-air – or, as in many academics' cases, they keep writing papers citing each other's scholarship and theoretical insights whilst boosting their own at the usual round of conferences. Yet, despite university application rates holding up so far (but see the following sections in this chapter) and exorbitant fees not putting off applicants to reduce numbers, particularly those from 'disadvantaged' backgrounds (but see Dorling, 2015), the Coalition's Higher Education Minister, David Willetts lost his 'great university gamble' (McGettigan, 2013). He admitted as much when he said that he did not expect to recover more than a third of what will add up to £330 billion of unpaid loans by 2046 (Ainley, 2015). The problem has been intensified by the repayment threshold remaining at £21,000. This suggests that the policy makers behind the scheme under-estimated, or were even unaware of, the depreciation in graduate salaries that were a consequence of the decline in 'graduate jobs'.

It is now likely the Conservative government will raise undergraduate fees or alter the terms of repayment or both. They have already announced that universities providing 'high quality teaching' will be allowed to raise their fees above the current £9,000 cap in line with inflation from 2017–18. Together with turning maintenance grants into loans, as mentioned earlier, this will add to the complex loan/insurance packages backing variously priced courses with different anticipated rates of return in employment that are the subject of speculative financial calculations – if buyers could be found for these 'financial products' to overcome the 'subprime' problems that have afflicted US SLABS (Student Loan Asset-Based Securities).

If fees were uncapped completely, Oxford, Cambridge and a handful of other 'top' universities would charge as much as they could, pricing themselves out of the system, although reluctant to forsake all state support whilst maintaining (perhaps as a condition of it) extensive bursaries and scholarships. This would leave universities which could not compete on price to go to the wall. Many would collapse into virtual learning centres in the way that franchised courses to overseas partners and campuses abroad already sustain home provision for many universities and faculties within them. 'Unbundling' could further unravel institutions. Management buyouts or corporate buy-ins are also possible, plus closure of under-recruiting/ researching departments and other cost-cutting measures. In the newer universities, more two-year 'degrees' could be taught over four terms a year. Private 'universities' and colleges offering more cut-price deals to state-funded students will be further encouraged despite repeated scandals over dubious standards. A free market would fragment what is left of a more or less coherent HE system but it is unlikely that the Tories will proceed directly to such a 'Big Bang' solution as the consequences would be dramatic and incalculable. Indeed, as things stand, Peter Scott warned of the possibility of *A* "perfect storm" as a result of "mounting turbulence" (2013: 54).

Although the likelihood of such turbulence is amplified by the market with 'students at the heart of the system' (DBIS, 2011), this is largely ignored by academic commentary, which focuses more on the commodifying effects of marketization – often upon academics themselves! However, this chapter argues that the most significant of these consequences of commodification lies in redefining large parts of HE to create a new single FE (or nominally FHE) sector that Palfreyman and Tapper call 'tertiary education (TE)' (2014: v). In reaction, more traditional approaches through academic disciplinarity have been asserted as a sign of 'distinction' (Bourdieu, 1982). However, as Rajani Naidoo (2003) pointed out, this only "protects the integrity of the academic enterprise . . . [by] unleashing new forms of elitism".

The last two decades have seen huge increases by 18–19 year olds in attendance at English HE, which has switched quickly from an elite to a mass participation system. As is the case with education and training in general, increased participation is explicitly related to changes in labour market opportunities as 'a good degree' is now essential for most secure employment. The Blair-Brown Labour governments set the ambitious target of half of 18–30 year olds being in HE by 2010, which was nearly achieved – for young women at least. Expanding university education was central to New Labour's "upskilling for globalisation" strategy (Leitch *Review of Skills, Prosperity for All in a Global Economy*, 2006). But the Coalition universities' minister, David Willetts, was under pressure to reduce student numbers, while also seeking to further differentiate by charging what the market would bear. This did not happen, however. Anxious not to be seen as providing an 'inferior product' but also because universities were now dependent on student fees to fund their courses, almost all higher education institutions announced they would charge the maximum fee capped at £9,000 by a compromise with the Lib Dems in the Coalition. Nevertheless, after an initial falling back, young people continued to enter higher education in large numbers in hopes of secure and at least semi-professional careers. In 2014, for the first time more than half a million students took up an offer of a place at a UK university. Most were English home students with women now making up 60 per cent of the undergraduate population – though this proportion would be reduced if courses in education and health were excluded. In 2015, notwithstanding some pick up in the economy, relentless propaganda for 'apprenticeships' and a demographic fall in numbers of 18–19-year-olds, the desperate competition between nearly all universities for fee-paying students made it easier than ever to get in and so more applied in the absence of any other alternative. (Also because this is the last year maintenance grants will be available – see the following section.)

Despite increased participation and because elite universities have not – at least for the time being – been able to differentiate themselves in the market through fee increases, institutions differentiate themselves in other ways. Russell universities require students to have top grades in at least two 'facilitating subjects', but from 2012, those universities have been gradually released from rationing the most qualified applicants amongst themselves. Consequently, all but two universities plus the London School of Economics (LSE) are in a frantic competition to cram in as many applicants as possible since their funding depends upon it! In other words, the universities poach students from one another, creaming off students who thought they were heading for more 'middling' universities but can use post-results 'clearing' to trade up – 'trade down' from the universities' point of view!

In "the endless chain of hierarchy and condescension that passes for a system [of higher education] in England" (Scott, 2015), those from lower socio-economic groups are sorted into the lower reaches of the student population to obtain lower-end 'graduate jobs' if they are lucky. Students and parents are well aware of the social hierarchy of subjects and institutions. Many can see that, as Michael Bailey and Des Freedman predicted in 2011,

> the UK's higher education system is to be transformed into a patchwork of academic supermarkets with, at one end, research-led Russell Group universities continuing to super-serve wealthier customers with a wide range of niche offerings while, at the other end, former polytechnics . . . will be forced to clear their shelves of distinctive or idiosyncratic goods and to focus on those products for which there is already a clearly defined (mass) market. All shoppers, meanwhile, will have to pay higher prices.
>
> (p.2)

A high level of applications for courses that are perceived to be directly vocational is understandable given the available alternatives and the increases in student fees. However, the definition of 'a graduate job' has become ever-more elastic, as this is a key indicator on which funding for universities depends. This is worse for the less academic post-1992 universities, but also includes many students who opt for science and technology subjects elsewhere only to find that, to avoid relegation to technician-level lab work, they have to proceed to post-graduation. This is further turning still larger parts of HE into FE and squeezing what remains of FE engineering, for example out of FE and into HE – through University Technical Colleges, for instance. At the same time, employers prefer graduates to apprentices for increasingly routinized technical work, whilst leading graduate employers continue to recruit more from a small number of elite institutions than they do from specific subject disciplines.

The distinction made by Silver (2004) is thus collapsed between 'going further' and 'going higher'; the logic of the former being a horizontal collection of equivalent competences, while that of the latter is vertical towards an abstracted overview from the top of an ivory tower. When she was principal of Lewisham College, Silver suggested that, at the same time as students at Lewisham's partner universities of Goldsmiths, Greenwich and South Bank aimed higher, they should also go further by attending Lewisham to acquire the practical competences employers always complain are missing in graduates who have only theoretical 'book knowledge' without practical application. This would combine 'higher' with 'further', education with training and 'deep' with 'surface' learning, or theory with practice on the polytechnic principle. What Silver called 'thick HE' would thus unite practical competence with generalized knowledge. Unfortunately, the idea never caught on! It could perhaps still find an opportunity to do so if HE were not reduced to FE in TE but combined with it (see Simmons, 2014).

Conclusion

Unfortunately, it is probably too late for this possibility to be realised in the foreseeable future. As Wolf writes, with 'the shift from "traditional" FE and the rise of work-based learning' (*o.c.*, p.26), 'universities are 'colonising areas of vocational education and training which were traditionally the preserve of . . . vocational schools or colleges' (p.74) with the result that 'more academically low achieving students are being recruited' (p.67). They sign on in hopes of a secure and at least semi-professional occupation for which the 2.1 or first-class degree now obtained by 70 per cent of graduates has become the essential qualification for interview if not employment (in the way that three A-levels were only a few years ago and five A-C GCSEs previously (Ainley & Allen, 2010; Ainley & Bailey, 1997). Widening participation is thus presented as professionalising the proletariat while disguising a proletarianisation of the professions as they are reduced towards the conditions of wage labour through the latest applications of new technology and new forms of contractual management that deskill and automate professional and managerial as well as technical and clerical non-manual occupations.

To indicate the differentiation of HE into a minority academic form of 'higher' education and the majority into Palfreyman and Tapper's tertiary education is not to denigrate 'lower-level' training but to recognize that 'higher-level' education is impossible without it. (Whereas it is quite possible – and increasingly common – to have training without education, e.g. in today's teacher training (Furlong, 2013)). It is also to recognize that the real division between traditional FE associated with the manual trades and elite HE associated with the 'non-manual' professions was one of social class. The divisions of knowledge and labour between these two classes of employed labour have broken down and the differentiation of a minority academic HE from a mass, 'vocational', nominal FHE reveals a new binarism in English HE. As a result, to quote from Wolf's conclusion,

> In post-19 education, we are producing vanishingly small numbers of higher technician level qualifications, while massively increasing the output of generalist bachelors degrees and low-level vocational qualifications. We are doing so because of the financial incentives and administrative structures that governments themselves have created, not because of labour market demand, and the imbalance looks set to worsen yet further. We therefore need, as a matter of urgency, to start thinking about post-19 funding and provision in a far more integrated way.
>
> (2015: 76)

One way in which to do this might be in terms of higher vocational pedagogy, though given its small uptake, higher-level apprenticeships is not yet providing an alternative to university entrance. The SFA recorded only 300 starts in 2011–12 by those under 19 (up to 600 for 2012–13) and only 2,400 by those 19–24. By comparison, A-levels continue to enrol around 300,000 young people each year. Though some may be lost, as noted earlier, claims that young people are deserting university for apprenticeships are therefore groundless.

University of Greenwich research (DBIS, 2013a) showed 53 per cent of advanced-level apprenticeships from a 2009–10 cohort had progressed via intermediate level (61 per cent for those under 19 and 60 per cent for those under 25), but with twice as many under 19-year-olds on intermediate apprenticeships.

However, this means that for the majority, there is no further progression, though as the number of advanced-level schemes continue to grow, rates of progression may too. The findings show low rates of progression from advanced level to HE. Rates fell to 8.1 per cent from 10.4 per cent in 2004–05, though they were higher for 17–19-year-olds (12.4 per cent). Those who did move on to HE were more likely to enrol in FE/Foundation degree courses than first degrees at university. Progression from advanced to higher-level apprenticeships was particularly low (2.5 per cent) – but this is understandable considering the limited number of these. Raikes (*o.c.*: 2015: 17) confirms higher-level apprenticeships up from 0.5 per cent of all apprentice starts in 2009–10 to 2.1 per cent since.

In these circumstances, given the persistence of the 'low-skill equilibrium' first identified by Finegold and Soskice in 1988 and without any serious attempt to 'rebalance' production in the deregulated, post-industrial, largely service-based economy of the UK, repeated efforts to cajole employers into subscribing to training and apprenticeships they do not want or need should be recognised as typical of the impression management that substitutes for government in a new market state. This is especially the case as employers have not welcomed the levy they regard the Conservatives as having unexpectedly imposed upon them. There has been consultation this autumn (2015), but the key point is that large employers will be required to make a payment as a percentage of payroll and then allowed to offset these contributions against apprentice training. Most employers will ensure their own training budgets get counted in this calculation. It could cause a shift in a few companies and public services away from recruiting graduates towards recruiting advanced or higher apprentices. However, the levy is due to be introduced alongside new digital discount vouchers in 2017, by which time government also hopes to have new apprenticeship qualifications in place. Three simultaneous reforms are being combined with a new government-sponsored IT system . . . Watch this space!

References

Ainley, P. (1999) *Learning Policy, Towards the Certified Society*. Basingstoke: Macmillan.
Ainley, P. (2015) English higher education: Fees are only the half of it! *Forum*, 57(1), 59–66.
Ainley, P. and Allen, M. (2010) *Lost Generation? New Strategies for Youth and Education*. London: Continuum.
Ainley, P. and Bailey, B. (1997) *The Business of Learning, Staff and Student Experiences of Further Education in the 1990s*. London: Cassell.
Allen, M. and Ainley, P. (2014) *Another Great Training Robbery or a Real Alternative for Young People? Apprenticeships at the Start of the Twenty-First Century*. London: Radicaled.
Avis, J. (2014) *Austerity and Modernisation, One Nation Labour – and Vocational Education and Training in England*. Oxford: Draft working paper presented as Research into Post-Compulsory Education and Training Conference.
Bailey, M. and Freedman, D. (eds.) (2011) *The Assault on Universities, A Manifesto for Resistance*. London: Pluto.

Bourdieu, P. (1982) *La Distinction: Critique sociale du jugement*. Paris: Editions de Minuit.
Brockmann, M., Clarke, L. and Winch, C. (2008) Knowledge, skills, competence: European divergences in vocational education and training (VET) – the English, German and Dutch cases. *Oxford Review of Education*, 34(5), xx.
Brynjolfsson, E. and McAfee, A. (2014) *The Second Machine Age, Work, Progress, and Prosperity in a Time of Brilliant Technologies*. New York: Norton.
Clark, T. and Heath, A. (2014) *Hard Times, Inequality, Recession, Aftermath*. London: Yale University Press.
Delebarre, J. (2015) *Apprenticeship Statistics for England 1996–2015*, Briefing Paper 06113.
Department for Business, Innovation and Skills. (2011) *Higher Education: Students at the Heart of the System*. London: DBIS.
Department for Business Innovation and Skills. (2013a) *Research Paper No. 107 Progression of Apprentices to Higher Education*. London: DBIS.
Department for Business Innovation and Skills. (2013b) *Research Paper No. 121 Apprenticeship Pay Survey*. London: DBIS.
Dorling, D. (2015) Six tends in university admissions. *Times Higher Education Supplement* 12 February 2015.
FE responds to autumn statement. *FE News* 5 December 2013, http://www.fenews.co.uk/fe-news/fe-sector-responds-to-autumn-statement
Finegold, D. and Soskice, D. (1988) The failure of training in Britain: Analysis and prescription. *Oxford Review of Economic Policy*, 4(3), 21–53.
Furlong, J. (2013) *Education – An Anatomy of the Discipline. Rescuing the University Project*. London: Routledge.
Gamble, A. (2009) *The Spectre at the Feast, Capitalist Crisis and the Politics of Recession*. Basingstoke: Palgrave Macmillan.
Harbour, P. (2015) *John Dewey and the Future of Community College Education*. London: Bloomsbury.
Hodgson, A. (ed.) (2015) *The Coming of Age for FE? Reflections on the Past and the Future Role of Further Education Colleges in England*. London: Institute of Education Press.
Hyland, T. (1994) *Competence, Education and NVQs*. London: Cassell.
Lansley, S. and Mack, J. (2015) *Breadline Britain, the Rise of Mass Poverty*. London: Oneworld.
Leitch, S. (2006) *Review of Skills: Prosperity for All in a Global Economy*. Norwich: HMSO.
Marx, K. (1971) *Capital* Vol. 1. London: Unwin.
McGettigan, A. (2013) *The Great University Gamble, Money, Markets and the Future of Higher Education*. London: Pluto.
Naidoo, R. (2003) Repositioning higher education as a global commodity: Opportunities and challenges for future sociology of education work. *The British Journal of Sociology of Education*, 24(2), 249–259.
Palfreyman, D. and Tapper, T. (2014) *Reshaping the University, the Rise of the Regulated Market in Higher Education*. Oxford: Oxford University Press.
Raikes, L. (2015) *Learner Drivers, Local Authorities and Apprenticeships*. London: IPPR.
Richard, D. (2012) *The Richard Review of Apprenticeships*. London: DBIS.

Roberts, K. (2010) *The End of the Long Baby-Boomer Generation? If So, What Next?* Liverpool University Department of Sociology, Unpublished paper.

Scott, P. (2013) The Coalition Government's reform of higher education: Policy formation and political process, in C. Callender and P. Scott (eds.) *Browne and Beyond, Modernizing English Higher Education*. London: Institute of Education Press, pp. 32–56.

Scott, P. (2015) *What Is a University? Talk at Premier of Film 'At Berkeley'*. London: Birkbeck College, 27 February 2015.

Shildrick, T., MacDonald, R., Webster, C. and Garthwaite, K. (2010) *The Low-Pay, No-Pay Cycle: Understanding Recurrent Poverty*. New York: Joseph Rowntree Foundation.

Silver, R. (2004) *14–19 Reform: The Challenge to HE*, Presentation to Higher Education Policy Institute at the House of Commons, 29 June.

Simmons, R. (2014) 'Sorry to have kept you waiting so long, Mr. Macfarlane': Further education after the coalition, in M. Allen and P. Ainley (eds.) *Education Beyond the Coalition, Reclaiming the Agenda*. London: Radicaled, pp. 82–105.

Smithers, A. (1997) A critique of NVQs and GNVQs, in M. Flude and S. Sieminski (eds.) *Education 14–19 Critical Perspectives*. London: Athlone, pp. 143–157.

Wolf, A. (2011) *Review of Vocational Education – The Wolf Report*. London: Department for Education.

Wolf, A. (2015) *Heading for the Precipice: Can Further and Higher Education Funding Policies be Sustained?* London: King's College London Policy Institute.

3 Merger talk in further education
Of whales and minnows, rhetoric and reality

Geoffrey Elliott

Context

It has become a truism that FE colleges are operating in an increasingly complex, difficult and turbulent environment. A key indicator of this is the sheer number of commentators who have characterised the sector as an 'industrial relations battlefield' (Shain & Gleeson, 1999) and highlighted the prevalence of human resource management strategies, drawing upon the most competitive business management models (Avis, 1998; Elliott & Hall, 1994; Leathwood, 2000; Randle & Brady, 1997). These shifts reflect the policy pattern of the determined introduction of a quasi-market economy in public services in the 1980s. In the wider education arena, this trend was marked by the 1988 Education Reform Act (DfES, 1988) and in post-compulsory education by the 1992 Further and Higher Education Act (DfE, 1992) that decoupled FE colleges from local authorities and at the same time gave colleges unprecedented autonomy, "repositioning FE in the marketplace" (Gleeson, 1996).

It would, however, be a mistake to think that a move to a managerialist control model has only taken place in colleges. Gleeson and Knights (2006: 282) are correct in seeing this turn in further education as part of neo-liberal reform in the public sector at large, that "places organisations in a continuous state of fending off impending crises, in circumstances where professionals rather than the audit culture can be held responsible for institutional failure". Gleeson *et al.* (2005: 454) highlight a consequence of this situation highly pertinent to our current discussion of mergers that "practitioners are conscious that in a climate of college mergers and reorganisations their jobs may be on the line". The theme of institutional failure is also highlighted by Goddard-Patel and Whitehead (2001:184) in one of the few identified case studies of a college failure, which argues that "without the very real threat of 'failure', the imposition of a quasi-market economy is ineffective in driving forward the entrepreneurial culture and the driven-down accountability which defines it."

It is the culture of failure prevalent in further education that has been responsible for eroding senior managers' self-confidence (Lumby, 2002), fostering performativity (Orr, 2009) and heralding the unprecedented wave of college restructuring and mergers during this last period (Welham, 2015). In this chapter, I suggest that this turmoil has significantly rebased colleges and their systems towards unstable, loosely coupled organisations, often unable or unwilling to resist market forces and that the critical factor in determining institutional success or failure is college leaders' ability and capacity to transform their organisation in response.

Investigating entrepreneurial leadership in the public sector, Currie *et al.* (2008) describe how staff would "tread warily in proposing and implementing change" and "blocked rather than supported innovation" in a context of sector reconfiguration, noting that those tendencies were particularly exacerbated in conditions where financial crisis and subsequent merger risk represented immediate threats to jobs. We should note here that it is this removal of a public-sector safety net for colleges that should lead us to speak of a market, rather than a quasi-market, operating in further education and that mergers, and consequently the closure of some colleges, are evidence of a *real* market at work (see Smith, 2007 for a discussion of markets and quasi-markets in an FE context in which a "funding driven attitude . . . dominated the management ethos of the College and its culture" p.56).

In their study of FE and the masculine/managerialist subject, Kerfoot and Whitehead (2000: 198) utilise the graphic metaphorical phrase 'Darwinian scramble for survival' to describe FE college ethos. What is interesting about this characterisation is that the Darwinian notion of the survival of the fittest clearly carries with it the idea of weaker FE colleges ceasing to exist – in effect that is what has happened through the mergers and dissolutions that have become commonplace in the sector.

Boundaries

The question of institutional boundaries, how they are made, sustained and changed is a neglected field of study in post-compulsory education. A notable exception is Bathmaker *et al.* (2008) who, in their study of FE colleges that offer HE, draw upon Mintzberg's (1979) notion of the professional bureaucracy to explain how these institutions maintain highly structured organisational systems through the "irresistible momentum of bureaucratisation" (Bathmaker *et al.*, 2008: 130). However, they note that as markets penetrate post-compulsory education, "operating environments are becoming more unstable, and arguably, less professional" (p.130). They introduce the idea of a "boundary paradox" (p.135), giving the example of dual sector colleges that may find duality associated on the one hand with dependence and difficulty due to validation and/or funding reliance on an HE partner, but with permissiveness and permeability on the other, so that through HE partnerships, FE colleges can extend the markets they work with and create progression agreements. Extending college boundaries in this way can be thought of as horizontal boundary management. Examples would be course progression agreements between colleges and universities (upward), access initiatives between colleges and schools (downward) and consortium arrangements for curriculum delivery, either vocational or academic (parallel). Much of the extant literature on boundaries in post-compulsory education focuses on these kinds of horizontal boundary maintenance and management, the benefits for learners and, frequently, the professional and identity concerns these relationships bring with them. On the other hand, there is a paucity of literature on vertical boundary management, where college leaders, for a variety of reasons, opt to dissolve and merge with another organisation, usually a larger and stronger college – hence our allusion to whales and minnows (actually a quotation from one of the participants in the research).

This contrast between barriers and possibilities is echoed in Withers' (1998: 55) findings from his study of FE Principals and incorporation, where "the post-incorporation college has increased constraints and opportunities which require managers to be increasingly far-sighted and inspirational in their role of leading their colleagues through the potential difficulties". Stoten goes further by stating there is "evidence to suggest that the 'institutional model' is increasingly under threat from alternative conceptions of organisational decision making and resource allocation" (Stoten, 2011: 156). These are crucial observations and ones which we strongly endorse, since all our work in this area demonstrates the centrality of leadership capacity to successfully negotiate adverse political and material circumstances. On the other hand, it can be argued that institutions are, of their nature, resistant to environmental influence, or at least robust in response to external threats. Most studies that take this line refer to a kind of institutional glue that operates through hierarchies, bureaucracy, management systems, institutional strategy and corporate culture as a sustaining force, enabling the institution to adapt and change but, crucially, survive turbulent change forces; however, few would go so far as Weber's notion of "stahlhartes Gehouse" or an 'iron cage' of bureaucracy, rationalism, modernism and capitalism, in short the modern world sustained by a concentrated mix of technical expertise, efficiency and accountability systems (Weber, 1905: 182).

Loose coupling

These intellectual traditions have permeated educational thinking to the extent that particular orthodoxies have become routinely absorbed into contemporary discourse as taken-for-granted assumptions. However, not to question the way in which organisations inter-relate and the balance of autonomy and agency on the one hand with constraint and regulation on the other is, I believe, to misrepresent the complex dynamic of social, political, cultural and economic interactions in post-modern societies. As a counter-thinker who challenged the prevailing technical-rationalist closed systems approach of his time, Karl Weick (1976) stands out as an educationalist contrarian. Writing 40 years ago, he challenged the dominant paradigm that analysed organisations and their systems through the Weberian lens of dense tight linkages. Instead, Weick adopted the idea of 'loose coupling' as a sensitising device to "tutor our judgement" (Stenhouse, 1979) so that we notice and question things that had previously been taken for granted. This idea of challenging researcher assumptions remains a crucial aspect of critical theory to this day and can help us understand different and differing orientations within a complex field. For us, the significant contribution of Weick's notion of loose coupling is that it draws attention to what he terms the 'sub-assemblies' that hold institutions together. These are predominantly grouped around the technical core of the organisation – what it is for, its scope, its personnel – and the authority of office – positions, responsibilities, rewards and sanctions. Loose coupling between these elements is held to account for unanticipated consequences, plans that go wrong and disconnect between staff and students or practitioners and managers. It is my contention that college leaders who fail to manage their boundaries well, and/or recognise that loose coupling is a highly significant variable influencing culture, ethos and realisation of institutional values, missions, goals and strategies, create a vacuum that, in today's highly politicised and deeply competitive landscape, begs to be filled. One of the strengths of Weick's analysis is that he combines theoretical speculation with everyday observation, for example drawing attention to the human tendency to over-rationalise behaviours and activities and "to attribute greater meaning, predictability, and coupling among them than in fact they have" (Weick, 1976: 9). The implication of this analysis is that college leaders who underestimate the power of external regulation or market forces and overestimate the solidity of their institutions with all their hierarchies and structures, lay themselves open to ambush and unanticipated consequences – set adrift in a loosely coupled and highly perilous educational marketplace. Finally, Weick directs us towards an appropriate research methodology for identifying and explaining loose coupling, viz., one that is contextually sensitive and rich in detail, exploring the lived experience of participants. He also highlights the benefit of comparative, longitudinal and case studies that can compare similar phenomena in different contexts.

In this study, the participants are an opportunity sample of 11 FE and sixth form college Principals in two English regions, including one private provider that was at the time of the research embedded in a community college. Many of the Principals had direct experience of leading mergers and merged institutions, or led colleges in close proximity and competition with them. The Principals were interviewed during the summer of 2013, a period that had seen a sharp acceleration in college mergers both locally and nationally. The focus of the wider study which prompted this chapter is specifically upon leadership, signalling a break with much of the research literature studying change in the post-compulsory education sector post-incorporation, which has concentrated on management rather than leadership. As Iszatt-White *et al.* (2011) have noted, although 'Over recent decades, the study of leadership has produced a swathe of theories, models and prescriptions for would-be leaders . . . There is little leadership wisdom, either original or adaptive, aimed at the post-compulsory learning and skills sector, however' (p.1). I believe there are a number of reasons for this. First, most of the literature on how colleges are run has identified what is frequently termed 'new managerialism' that is characterised in overwhelmingly negative terms, associated with strict financial management, efficient use of resources, extensive use of quantitative performance indicators, development of consumerism and the discipline of the market, accountability and the assertion of 'the manager's right to manage' (Randle & Brady, 1997: 230).

Second, with some exceptions, including the work of the Centre for Excellence in Leadership at Lancaster (see, for example Jameson & Andrews, 2008) and Jameson's earlier work with FE Principals (2006a), there has been relatively little written about good leadership in post-compulsory education aside from a paucity of ethnography and case studies of well-led institutions and a legacy of educational leadership work that is of questionable veracity that overly emphasises personal aptitudes and styles rather than leadership in situated educational contexts, or in any sense transformational.

Third, much of the literature in this area locates FE management shifts within the wider context of public-sector management, even though since 1992 further education colleges have been incorporated institutions, outwith local authority control – albeit still dependent upon government contracts for their principal funding source (Currie *et al.*, 2008; Gleeson & Knights, 2006).

Fourth, there has been an enduring dualism, both in the literature and in practice, between managerialism and professionalism, signifying a conceptual separation between tutors, lecturers and other practitioners on the one hand and those in senior positions, seldom conceived as practitioners, on the other, resulting in an unfortunate and often unquestioned taken-for-granted cultural landscape of FE in which two tribes go to war, in other words, a simplistic dualism between managers and the managed.

Having laid these theoretical foundations, we can now explore how a group of FE Principals imagine and experience organisational maintenance, change, transformation and, ultimately, survival. These are big questions, since institutional condition, readiness and direction has a huge impact upon the human condition in those organisations, and one of the principal skills of those who lead is to manage transformation in ways that do not fracture and disrupt educational outcomes (Elliott, 2013).

Metaphors

It has been correctly deduced that metaphors in use are an invaluable way of uncovering ethos, culture (Semino, 2008) and hidden assumptions (Jameson, 2006b), and we felt that a study of those in use by our sample of Principals (referred to as P1, P2, etc.) was likely to be especially illuminating in the highly charged political environment of contemporary post-compulsory education. They frequently made use of metaphors to characterise the economic and policy environment they found themselves in. In particular, we were interested in how metaphorical language might direct us to the questions of the day in their thinking about the possibility of merger. We surmised that this in turn might direct us to critical themes for our analysis of the reality and rhetoric of merger in current post-compulsory education.

The most significant metaphor in place throughout the interview data in our study is that of the market in education. This manifested itself overwhelmingly as both positive and negative in the minds of most Principals. For example a negative consequence is the unnecessary duplication of the curriculum offer.

A positive consequence is the capacity to compete and grow the college business, sometimes through merger, of course.

Formerly in England, FE colleges were governed and macro-managed by the local education authority in which they happened to be situated. A process of curriculum planning, for what was at the time known as advanced and non-advanced FE, was overseen by the authority officer responsible for the sector, involving the Principals and senior teams of the colleges concerned. Following incorporation of the sector in 1992, these processes were abandoned and colleges were left to position themselves in an increasingly competitive educational marketplace (Elliott & Crossley, 1994).

The most frequent metaphorical allusion our sample of Principals made was that of fighting and conflict and survival. P1 states, "the sixth form colleges . . . have fought off two or three merger proposals", and maintains that the college has "been able to very much survive because of our quality and popularity". P2 speaks of having to "weather the financial storm and come out the other end stronger". P3, talking about the local context, tries to understand "the relationship of the whale to the minnow" and suggests that sometimes "being eaten is a good thing you know, maybe". P3 presents a rationale for seeking partnerships as 'obviating a threat', and characterises the growth of multi-academy trusts and teaching schools as "a Jurassic Park with a lot of big beasts developing". P7 uses a similar idea: "colleges either get themselves into trouble from a financial perspective or from an Ofsted/quality perspective, then other colleges will be predatory and take them over".

All the Principals used the notion of stakeholders to describe different groups affected by their college, including students, employers and the community. In talking about mergers, their language frequently draws upon an economic lexicon, including words and phrases such as "diseconomies of scale" (P4), "funding driven" (P6), "financial failure" (P8), "financial storm" (P1), "increasing their profitability" (P7), "financial mess" (P2), "invest in the right people" (P4), "driven by funding" (P10), "adjust your base as any other business would do" (P11). Often, the language used to describe the consequences of merger revolves around power and control: "The drawbacks are that you lose focus, you lose identity, you lose control" (P10). Often, Principals talked in terms of processes and change being driven: "to drive that skills agenda" (P2), "driving the future shape of educational pathways" (P4), "we are financially driven" (P5), strategic options review is "partly driven by funding being decreased year on year". In the next sections, we explore in more detail some of the themes underlying the range of market-oriented metaphors that emerge in the interviews

Sustainability

Institutional size and finance – often expressed in terms of sustainability – are a continually recurring theme for the college leaders in our sample. The first Principal we spoke to alerted us to how prevalent this concern was: "you will hear this from some of the other FE people you speak to that there is a critical size of budget for an FE college, certainly" (P1). Some of the institutions led by our sample were small general FE colleges, which one Principal judged "in terms of long-term sustainability, you know, I don't think it can remain as a standalone institution" (P6). Sometimes the argument to grow through merger was expressed in terms of economies of scale:

> some of the facilities are quite expensive so for them the economies of scale and efficient use of resources are a big incentive plus obviously all the cross college cost centres such as HR, finance and so on can be centralised for them, it's a big issue.
>
> (P2)

This Principal actually put a figure on the minimum turnover believed required to survive the new funding arrangements for FE: "colleges with a turnover of less than £30M are looking to work together to create something bigger than that because they believe there will be a chance of coping better with the circumstances we are in" (P2). Sometimes, though very much in the minority of cases, financial savings were associated with an improved educational offer. P10 was in no doubt that

> merger is being driven by funding because I think in FE funding per student has been going down, certainly for institutions like us which have quite a high level of funding because we do very full programmes and they're expensive programmes because you've got workshops and things like that.

Aware that merging in order to strengthen a college's financial position can appear to be a negative motivation, P5 urges caution in interpreting what some college leaders say about merger: "people are very quick to say, oh it's all about developing services and strategic alliances and reaching communities, but I don't really believe a lot of the rhetoric around that, I think it's predominantly financial". Hence the allusion in our title to rhetoric and reality. Another Principal also urged caution in interpreting other Principals' motives in partnerships: "their real objective isn't to work in partnership, their real objective is to try and see if they can engineer a situation where they can take that college over, that's all it would be" (P7).

Quality

Quality, within a highly regulated standards system such as Ofsted, is of course very closely linked to finance and funding, since poor inspection outcomes are inevitably sooner or later associated with reduced funding. One Principal argued that it is predominantly failure in one of these areas that brought about college mergers:

I think too many mergers have been done where, there's been an element of failure, or financial, so it'll be quality failure or financial failure and I can think of very few instances of two colleges coming together for real strategic reasons.

(P8)

For another Principal, merger creates a danger of deflection from the college's mission and purpose, not least the quality of its offering:

there are plenty of colleges that seem to have merged and grown enormously and then lost the focus on what colleges are there to do which is teach, teach young people and so that they can succeed in their studies and there's, so much energy goes into all the corporate, the changes to the corporate services that they can lose out on quality and there's some very good, if you know anything about FE, there is some very good examples of disastrous Ofsted results in very large colleges where there has been a lot of merger activity.

(P5)

Finance and quality are similarly conflated in another Principal's mind: "what you've got is a lot of colleges being in financial difficulty, sometimes in quality difficulty, and the two are not always unrelated, who are saying this can't go on, help, how do we get out of this mess?" (P2). Similarly, another Principal observes:

The other motive which has been behind at least one merger of two sixth form colleges has been quality issues where financially the college which was significantly underperforming was financially reasonably stable but it was management and quality that were the issues there and the best way for that college to improve was to merge with a much much stronger, reasonable local college.

(P1)

Community

By community we mean the local community served by the college. As noted earlier, we were alerted by some Principals to a tendency for their colleagues to ascribe higher motives than the business considerations that appear to be driving mergers. It is likely that the current requirement for colleges that wish to merge to carry out a local consultation process also prompts foregrounding of local concerns. However, it was not possible for this study to test how genuine expressions of community interest were. What is clear though is that the subject was frequently raised by our sample, with almost every Principal identifying community interest as a core concern in considering the future strategic direction of the college. For the following two Principals, the interest of learners should be predominant: "For me the motive (for merger) ought to be improving quality and improving the opportunities for students" (P1). P2 concurs: "the primary issue always has to be to look at what the organisation is for, and how you can fulfil that . . . it should always be driven by improving what's available for the people to learn irrespective of anything else". Another Principal emphasised the importance of locality, "Our focus is about providing a very strong local presence" (P4), whilst another inserted an historical dimension: "the danger (of merger) is the bigger colleges then stop serving the community, you know, in the holistic way that it did in the past" (P5). A number of Principals alluded to the disruption that mergers often bring about:

> it's a lot harder than people think to bring, you know, bring two different organisations together and there can be a lot of sort of dislocation that comes about through that and I suppose people perhaps spend too much time focusing on the mechanics of the merger and perhaps take their eyes off the ball in terms of, you know, the real objectives of the organisation.
>
> (P9)

Another Principal concurs: "mergers are very disruptive, you know, they really turn the place upside down, so you've got to have a really good reason for doing it" (P10). Disruption also applies to the curriculum offer: "the downside would be that as a result of merger that services are taken away, the provision is stripped or placed elsewhere" (P6). One Principal expressed the strongest opposition to merger of our entire sample:

> I don't see any short-term, medium term benefits actually. I think they are immensely destabilising for an organisation. Colleges are basically local organisations. And now if there's no purpose to that organisation then you need to address that and rationalise the organisation. If there is, then get on with it and do it really. Merging is probably avoiding the core issues. If an organisation, isn't financially, educationally viable when . . . how can someone else change that?
>
> (P11)

Policy

All of the Principals in the sample referred at some point to education as a market, suggesting that colleges are now more subject to market forces, which had, for them, both positive and negative elements. For following Principal, there will be casualties created by the new more flexible arrangements that lower barriers to merger:

> So, this government believes in market forces, so we are moving into a market forces world in education of this type and there will be blood, you know,

there will be, because there are organisations with the aspiration to do it, who either won't make it or they'll make it.

(P3)

Another Principal fully embraced the freedoms and potential for joint working and collaboration that he identified as associated with a market in education: "a federated model, I could see that being interesting in terms of an umbrella for shared services for HE/FE/UTC's other academies, could come under that umbrella and I think there are, to get efficiencies and economy, yes" (P4). Similarly, another Principal welcomed the new policy context in which the former power of government agencies and quangos is reduced:

> what happens is that the college, that the new scheme, the new system is that the governing board of the college will look for appropriate partners, so there is no, in days gone by some governing agency used to broker and point score and interfere and now it's really the colleges strike up their own relationships themselves, so there are other opportunities.
>
> (P5)

Another Principal suggested that where government had influence its policy is confused:

> In five years, a hundred colleges have gone, and I don't know any of them have been closed down so therefore they have been merged . . . But this is where the policy and strategy is contradictory because on the one hand government will say colleges are too big and then, that's not what they want, but on the other hand they're quite happy for colleges to be taken over or merged when there's an issue.
>
> (P7)

Another Principal could identify no policy direction at any level influencing college mergers: "We're talking national policies and things really, I don't think there's any cunning educational plan, because, to be honest, I think what we're seeing is the lack of any sort of regional or local educational plan" (P10). For another Principal, worth quoting at length, the policy direction has led to a somewhat chaotic FE landscape:

> So I think that there is a massive political imperative and push towards colleges to use their flexibilities and freedoms and models have been suggested, but some of these models mean losing sovereignty and losing your franchise . . . Yes I think, well, locally, I suppose locally and nationally, we are going through pretty horrendous funding cuts which we are having to look at, but also the freedoms and flexibilities, what concerns me is that the landscape could become very cluttered and confused because it seems to me that academies, UTC's, free schools, can set up almost at the drop of a hat and I think

it's sort of like, slight government rhetoric gone a little bit mad, because it's unplanned and I think we might find ourselves in 5 years' time looking back thinking how on earth did we allow that to happen?

(P8)

Control

Our final category earns its place by virtue of the number of times that Principals' ambition and desire for control is raised by our sample. Few were open enough to ascribe this motive for merger to themselves, but many identified the trait in their peers; as one Principal puts it:

> I, there are lots of reasons why people have come together in different forms across the sector. Some I think are sensible and I can see why it makes a lot of sense and it adds a lot of value to the locality, others I suspect are more . . . less philanthropic and more about self-interest and making money. And that's not always necessarily . . . I think is . . . always leading to the best use of public money.
>
> (P4)

In another Principal's comments we can infer an acquisitive style of leadership: "There's some aggressive organisations around who are quite . . . who have a strategic point in life to merge and acquire other organisations which just jolts behaviour" (P11). Another Principal talked more directly in terms of

> people's personal ambition, I think has something to do . . . the view of the . . . I mean the Principal is very powerful in the view of the board, but the view of the Principal and the senior staff, particularly the Principal about what . . . about what he or she wants to achieve, and I think there is a personal, erm, people have different views about what might or might not succeed, so that, I think the personal thing is, and the personal ambition, whatever that, whether that's right or wrong, or neither.
>
> (P5)

Another Principal, worth quoting at length, was openly frank:

> The drawbacks (of being merged) are the obvious ones, all the reasons why you wouldn't do it. They are loss of local control, loss of local decision making, the risk that you don't any longer control your own purse strings and it's all of those things around control. This is a conversation which we've had endlessly over the last few months. We could talk all day about that. We have an organisation that we believe we are developing in that way that we've always wanted it to develop and sometimes we get it right and sometimes we get it wrong. This college is what I and my team have created it to be and therefore the prospect of going to another organisation and saying actually

we will become part of you, there's all that drawback that you risk losing all of that, you risk losing the say so.

(P2)

Conclusion

A question frequently posed in the literature (see, for example Abramson *et al.*, 1996; Colley *et al.*, 2014; Macbeth *et al.*, 1995) is collaborate or compete? The tension is well expressed by two of the Principals in our sample:

> There is no way in terms of where you are looking at your mission and values and your strategic objectives and then you look at what's happening in the funding landscape, you are not going to achieve that by maintaining your historical shape, it's impossible. Therefore, the key reasons why people have looked at it now and are looking at it now is that they are being forced to look at it. I mean I think that's a shame because I think the arguments I have put to you about why there should be, say in the [Place name] context it was a suboptimal structure in terms of too many small organisations, that applied before the financial pressures, but for other reasons people, when they are not forced to look at things, tend to just stick to the status quo, often because it does require a strategic vision and a drive that says you can be better together and you can move in terms of ambition, but you've always got the problems, be it individual Principals' self-interest, governors and local community narrow self-interest, rather than bigger picture, that's fact. That's a fact, I've worked in six/seven regions and it's the same everywhere. It's not just something you'd find in [Place name]. The reality is, the answer to the question is simple, why there is more activity at the moment is because people who should have and could have looked to work collaboratively in the past didn't because they didn't have to. Now they are having to and in particular a lot of smaller and small/medium sized colleges are having to look at it as a way of surviving.

(P4)

> I think the difficulty is that one ends up looking at all of these things as things which are competing with each other for the same people and I think if there is a way of looking at it that says we are actually all in the same business of creating skilled people to do those things that need to be done then that's got to be a more positive way of looking at it, but that's a bit pie in the sky sometimes, that's the situation with, that's why I suppose the FE sector swings from collaboration to competition every few years and I think when there is plenty of money about you collaborate in a friendly way, when there's no money about you either compete hell for leather or you collaborate in the sense that you say, ok if you can't beat them, join them.

(P2)

There is a strong sense in these extracts, and throughout the conversations we had with Principals, that merger distorts the educational process to the extent that collaboration and cooperation are fundamental to good educational thinking and practice. This view is stated very explicitly by the following Principal:

> The whole point of merging is the rationalisation process. So it must drip out cost. It must drip out core activities and either outsource them or use other approaches. So general uncertainty, lack of focus as a corporate body as a sort of separate entity and basically a great danger of lack of engagement with local people, schools, partners et cetera because it's more, more distant and that local knowledge is quite powerful. I'm not a proponent of that.
>
> (P11)

This image that merger 'drips out' core activities is a powerful one and echoes other metaphors employed, as we have seen in this chapter, to depict a sector that is imbued with predatory behaviour and threat. Our Principals viewed merger as a clear consequence of the introduction of a real market in further education and as a vivid expression of business interests prevailing to the cost of educational ones, insofar as learners' interests appeared to many to be put in danger by the loss of community locus and responsiveness. All this illustrates well how loosely coupled organisations in the FE sector have become and are, as many of our Principals feared, losing sight of mission and educational values in the search for financial stability or expansion through merger. There is a real sense in which many of these leaders felt highly constrained by the political and funding environment of FE, to the point where merger may have seemed almost inevitable. We believe this lends support to the assertion by McTavish (2006) that, in part, because of the local nature of FE there is a "strategic capacity gap" within the sector (p.425).

Our thinking about institutional boundaries, and the idea of loosely coupled systems, has alerted us to the critical importance of effective leadership in steering educational organisations through hard times. In particular, we need to go on to explore how leaders can bring about transformation in their colleges without dissolution. There is no sign that merger activity is slowing in the FE sector, quite the reverse. The model of large college groups being established with an annual turnover approaching £50 million seems likely to become more common. From the evidence of this study, commercial success in a marketised FE landscape can carry a high cost of reduced community engagement, fewer educational opportunities and severing of formerly collaborative partnership arrangements. In so far as these elements have for many years framed the core business of FE colleges, and unless college Principals can lead effectively and transformatively, we fear for the future of the sector as an engine of widening participation and educational opportunity.

Acknowledgement

The author is grateful for the invaluable contribution of Ms Gemma Thomas, Research Assistant for this project.[1]

Note

1 Since the completion of this study, three of the colleges led by Principals in the sample group have merged and a fourth is carrying out a government Department of Business, Innovation and Skills (BIS) Strategic Options Review.

References

Abramson, M., Bird, J. and Stennett, A. (eds.) (1996) *Further and Higher Education Partnerships: The Future for Collaboration*. Buckingham: Open University Press.

Avis, J. (1998) (Im)possible dream: Post-Fordism, stakeholding and post-compulsory education. *Journal of Education Policy*, 13(2), 251–263.

Bathmaker, A., Brooks, G., Parry, G. and Smith, D. (2008) Dual-sector further and higher education: Policies, organisations and students in transition. *Research Papers in Education*, 23(2), 125–137.

Colley, H., Chadderton, C. and Nixon, L. (2014) Collaboration and contestation in further and higher education partnerships in England: A Bordieusian field analysis. *Critical Studies in Education*, 55(2), 104–121.

Currie, G., Humphreys, M., Ucbasaran, D. and McManus, S. (2008) Entrepreneurial leadership in the English public sector: Paradox or possibility? *Public Administration*, 86(4), 987–1008.

Department for Education (DfE). (1992) *Further and Higher Education Act*. London: HMSO.

Department of Education and Science (DfES). (1988) *Education Reform Act*. London: HMSO.

Elliott, G. (2013) Critical practice leadership in post-compulsory education. *Educational Management, Administration and Leadership*, first published on-line on 7 November2013.http://ema.sagepub.com/content/early/2013/11/06/174114 3213494891.

Elliott, G. and Crossley, M. (1994) Beyond incorporation: Policy and practice. *Educational Management and Administration*, 21(3), 188–197.

Elliott, G. and Hall, V. (1994) FE Inc.: Business orientation in further education and the introduction of human resource management. *School Organisation*, 14(1), 3–10.

Gleeson, D. (1996) Postcompulsory education in a post-industrial and post-modern age, in J. Avis, M. Bloomer, G. Esland, D. Gleeson and P. Hodkinson (eds.) *Knowledge and Nationhood*. London: Cassell, pp. 83–104.

Gleeson, D., Davies, J. and Wheeler, E. (2005) On the making and taking of professionalism in the further education workplace. *British Journal of Sociology of Education*, 26(4), 445–460.

Gleeson, D. and Knights, D. (2006) Challenging dualism: Public professionalism in 'troubled' times. *Sociology*, 40(2), 277–295.

Goddard-Patel, P. and Whitehead, S. (2001) The mechanics of 'failure' in further education: The case of Bilston community college. *Policy Studies*, 22(3/4), 181–195.

Iszatt-White, M., Randall, D., Rouncefield, M. and Graham, C. (2011) *Leadership in Post-Compulsory Education*. London: Continuum.

Jameson, J. (2006a) *Leadership in Post-Compulsory Education: Inspiring Leaders of the Future*. London: Routledge.

Jameson, J. (2006b) The authenticity of metaphors of transformational leadership in further education. http://www.leeds.ac.uk/educol/documents/157451.htm (Accessed 11 November 2015).

Jameson, J. and Andrews, M. (2008) Trust and leadership in the lifelong learning sector. *CEL Research Report*. Centre for Excellence in Leadership/Inspire Learning Ltd., Lancaster Management School, University of Lancaster. http://www.lancaster.ac.uk/lums/lsis/download-centre/he-research/ (Accessed 31 May 2016)

Kerfoot, D. and Whitehead, S. (2000) Keeping all the balls in the air: FE and the masculine/managerialist subject. *Journal of Further and Higher Education*, 24(2), 183–201.

Lancaster CEL Research Programme. (2007–2008) https://www.lancaster.ac.uk/media/lancaster-university/content-assets/documents/lums/lsis/r11.pdf (Accessed 11 November 2015).

Leathwood, C. (2000) Happy families? Pedagogy, management and discourses of control in the corporatised further education college. *Journal of Further and Higher Education*, 24(2), 163–182.

Lumby, J. (2002) Distributed leadership in colleges: Leading or misleading? Keynote paper presented at the *BELMAS Annual Conference*, Birmingham, September.

Macbeth, A., McCreath, D. and Aithinson, J. (eds.) (1995) *Collaborate or Compete? Educational Partnerships in a Market Economy*. London: The Falmer Press.

McTavish, D. (2006) Further education management strategy and policy. *Educational Management, Administration and Leadership*, 34(3), 411–428.

Mintzberg, H. (1979) *The Structuring of Organizations*. Englewood Cliffs, NJ: Prentice-Hall.

Orr, K. (2009) Performativity and professional development: The gap between policy and practice in the English further education sector. *Research in Post-Compulsory Education*, 14(4), 479–489.

Randle, K. and Brady, N. (1997) Further education and the new managerialism. *Journal of Further and Higher Education*, 21(2), 229–239.

Semino, E. (2008) *Metaphor in Discourse*. Cambridge: Cambridge University Press.

Shain, F. and Gleeson, D. (1999) Under new management: Changing perceptions of teacher professionalism and policy in the further education sector. *Journal of Education Policy*, 14(4), 445–462.

Smith, R. (2007) Of 'Duckers and divers', mice and men: The impact of market fundamentalism in FE colleges post-incorporation. *Research in Post-Compulsory Education*, 12(1), 53–69.

Stenhouse, L. (1979) Case study in comparative education: Particularity and generalisation. *Comparative Education*, 15(1), 5–11.

Stoten, D. (2011) Envisaging new education provision: Innovative organisation in the age of new modernism. *Research in Post-Compulsory Education*, 16(2), 155–171.

Weber, M. 1905 (1992) *The Protestant Ethic and the Spirit of Capitalism*. T. Parsons (trans.), London: Routledge.

Weick, K. (1976) Educational organizations as loosely coupled systems. *Administrative Science Quarterly*, 21(1), 1–19.

Welham, H. (2015) Cuts, competition and Ofsted – A lethal cocktail driving colleges to merge. http://www.theguardian.com/education/2015/feb/18/cuts-competition-ofsted-colleges-merge. (Accessed 11 November 2015).

Withers, B. (1998) The experience of incorporation 1993–95: Principals' impressions. *Research in Post-Compulsory Education*, 3(1), 39–56.

4 Groundhog Day again

Making sense of a complicated mess: HIVE-PED research on FE student and apprentice progression to higher education in England

Jill Jameson, Hugh Joslin and Sharon Smith

Introduction

The metaphor 'Groundhog Day' was used in relation to the VET sector by Professors Christopher Winch and Terry Hyland in 2007 in the book *A Guide to the Vocational Education and Training Sector* (Winch & Hyland, 2007: 11), part of a series on FE edited and commissioned by the first author (Jameson, 2007). Chris argued that the FE sector was stuck in a continual time loop in which there was never any escaping from the complex dysfunctionalities caused by endless disempowering top-down policy changes marked by a lack of respect and understanding of the true purpose and mission of higher vocational education. Despite endless policy and restructuring changes during the intervening 12 years from 2004 to 2016, there seems to have been little real underlying transformation from this basic theme. Indeed, as Karr wrote in 1849, *"plus ça change, plus c'est la même chose"* (the more things change, the more they stay the same (Karr, 1849: vi).

In the film *Groundhog Day*, the nightmarish time loop of ever-repeating days in Punxsutawney finally ends in a harmonious resolution when Phil breaks through his embittered sense of victimhood and isolation, developing compassion, understanding and expertise in becoming a highly skilled, authentic and optimistic human being (Solman, 1993). In short, Phil becomes a more genuine version of the person he truly is. The 'Groundhog Day' metaphor summarises the paralysing entrapment of Phil's repeating journey through time in a continuously re-run day which he is condemned to re-live until he can break through the cycle of re-occurring dysfunctionalities, misfits and resentments. Phil gradually begins to learn how to live as an authentic person, overcoming his selfishness and learning how to listen and be generous.

Groundhog Day can also be used as a metaphor to sum up the marginalised past history of the further and higher vocational education and training sector, in which the supercomplex overbureaucratisation (Barnett, 2000; Caiden, 1985) of the qualifications, MIS and funding systems has densely obscured understanding and obstructed learner progression pathways. Like Phil, those in the sector struggling with apparently endlessly repeating winter days of austerity and exhausting demands are eager for breakthroughs that enable the system to work.

Applying a unique methodology to facilitate understanding of progression by undertaking the challenging task of linking actual learner data from ILR and HESA records, a University of Greenwich research team investigated the progression of different types of learners from FE and apprenticeship provision into HE. Working with support from HESA and Higher Education Funding Council for England (HEFCE), the team devised a means of matching ILR records with HESA datasets to identify and analyse data on college students and apprentices progressing to HE in FE and to university over time. The most recent reports of this work are Smith *et al.*, 2015a, 2015b, 2015c. In collaboration with other experts (Evans *et al.*, 2011; Fuller & Unwin, 2012; Parry & Thompson, 2002; Parry *et al.*, 2012; Carter, 2010), this research is now being further developed as part of an ESRC-funded research seminar series on Higher Vocational Education and Pedagogy (HIVE-PED). To break through the apparently impenetrable impasse separating the complex ILR and HESA systems recording FE, HE and apprenticeships participation is to enable local systems to work more coherently. The team sought to understand progression rates, achievements and trends of specific learner cohorts by mode and course in non-prescribed and prescribed HE over time and to analyse these against demographic and regional data. The resulting patterns were then mapped against the existing literature on progression using a sense-making framework (Weick, 2012).

This paper provides an overview of the findings of ground-breaking progression data, demonstrating how this might be utilised to provide benefit for learners and providers, reducing the potential for a long-term future 'chaotic landscape' in FE-HE (Sherlock & Perry, 2013) and increasing opportunities for greater understanding, learner empowerment and social equality through expedited progression to higher study. The evidence from longitudinal research is then examined to consider the case for 'sense-making' in what has for decades been regarded as an overly complex system:

> I see no evidence, despite decades of "bureaucracy-busting taskforces" et al. that external bureaucracy has improved. Civil servants seem to delight in creating ever-more impenetrable funding mechanisms which would be far more effective if simpler.
>
> (Policy Consortium, 2014)

Just as the incessant nature of ongoing top-down policy changes to post-compulsory education have led to complaints that the sector has been 'raining policy' continuously for decades (Hillier & Jameson, 2003; Jameson & Hillier, 2003; Jameson & Hillier, 2008), so the over-complexity of the post-compulsory and FE systems in England has been critiqued, as graphically illustrated by Frank Coffield in his third and final inaugural professorial lecture in 2006 in the following structural diagram:

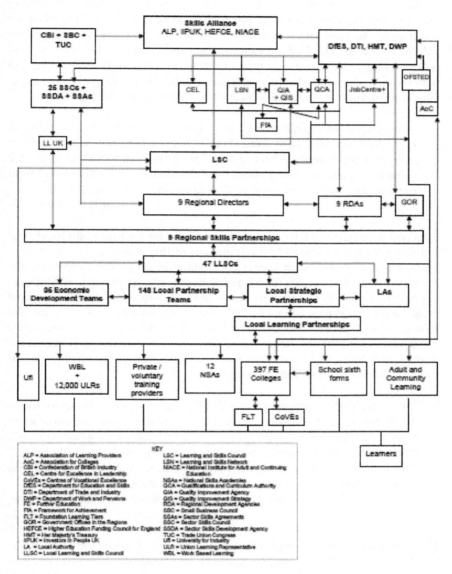

Figure 4.1 The post-compulsory education system in England (Coffield, 2006)

An updated version of this figure is reproduced on pages 16–17 of *Improving Learning, Skills and Inclusion*, published by Routledge in 2008.

Coffield's diagram attempts to depict all the different interconnected parts of the 'post-compulsory education system in England' in 2006, an almost hopelessly convoluted Sisyphean task, bearing in mind the number of rapid policy changes likely to rain on the sector during any one time period, necessitating thereby a restart as soon as one finished, in the same manner as if we attempted continuously to paint and repaint the Forth Bridge: a lifelong learning process indeed. In that lecture, Coffield sums up the convergence of the issues of rapid policy change and increasing complexity in what he termed the 'learning and skills sector', otherwise called post-compulsory education and/or FE and/or lifelong learning and/or vocational education and training and/or FE-HE:

> The processes of change have been complex, uneven, dynamic, ambiguous, hotly contested and often contradictory. Policies have not only evolved or been radically altered, as Secretaries of State and senior civil servants have come and gone, but some policies were abandoned, while others were from the start internally inconsistent or flatly contradicted existing policies.
> (Coffield, 2006: 2–3)

Concerns about the bewildering complexity of this system led to calls for change and simplification, which resulted in numerous further policy modifications. This resulted in a 2008 House of Commons Committee government report on the need to improve and simplify the FE and skills system (The Innovation, Universities, Science and Skills Committee, House of Commons, 2008) and the National Audit Office recommendations in 2011 on *Reducing Bureaucracy in Further Education in England* (NAO, 2011). Yet, despite these initiatives, the overly bureaucratic and complex nature of the system seems to have largely stayed the same or even worsened since that time. The 2008 report offered observations about comments from staff in the sector:

> We heard pleas from practitioners for simplification. Colourful phrases were used about how training and skills provision looks to those who come into contact with it: "a pig's ear or a dog's breakfast", "a very complex duplicating mess", "almost incomprehensible", "astonishing complexity and perpetual change." One witness told us that "I do not think there is an employer in the land who understands what the elements of the new system are, particularly pre-19".
> (The Innovation, Universities, Science and Skills Committee, House of Commons, 2008: 3)

The Commons committee report therefore commented somewhat despairingly: "Taking the national, regional and sectoral complexities together it seems to us that much of this system is impenetrable to everyone apart from possibly a few civil servants and a handful of academics" (The Innovation, Universities, Science and Skills Committee, House of Commons, 2008: 3). Yet despite, ostensibly, six years' work in the interim to improve this situation, progress seems to have gone backwards yet again, with numerous additional policy changes complicating the FE landscape even more in 2014. As Lynne Sedgmore, executive director of the 157 Group, recently said, "Unnecessary bureaucracy can result as an unintended consequence of policy initiatives" (Whittaker, 2014).

Unintended consequences result from a failure to see the wider and longer-term systemic implications that arise from multiple smaller actions. Individual policy makers have for decades played about with the post-compulsory education system with a series of short-term fixes, leaving a legacy of broken bits of restructurings and old 'new initiatives' which have been abandoned or left hanging, cluttering the landscape as policy makers moved on to the next job or policy agenda. Ruth Silver identified this 'malleability' of the sector in an interview on leadership and management in post-compulsory education in 2005: "FE is the adaptive layer in the education system" (Jameson, 2006: 54). The post-compulsory education landscape, including further, vocational, apprenticeships and FE-HE provision, is, as a result, a tangled bureaucratic nightmare, a Kafkaesque wilderness of broken parts, with "a very complex duplicating mess" of progression routes that defy ready understanding.

Supercomplexity of the national picture on learner progression

The supercomplexity and excessive bureaucratisation of the further and higher vocational education qualifications, progression and knowledge system, including apprenticeship programmes in England (Barnett, 2000; NAO, 2011), has therefore, inter alia, densely obscured understanding of the national picture on qualifications, learner data and progression from FE and apprenticeship provision to HE. Progression of learners between these sectors is complicated by different funding routes, dissimilar data collection systems and a highly dense mixture of vocational qualifications delivered across multiple different systems in a variety of organisations. For example as Alison Fuller identified in her BERA presentation in 2014, there are more than 5,000 individual apprenticeship pathways, but a disappointingly smaller number lead to clear employment outcomes (Fuller & Unwin, 2014).

Different routes to HE: New research on learner progression joins the dots

In 1998, the New Labour government introduced the principle of fees and student loans into the system of HE in England. In 2012, the UK Conservative–Liberal Democrat Coalition government took this principle to its logical conclusion and placed the problem of funding of HE squarely on its main consumers, students, raising tuition fees to their highest level, with most HE institutions opting for the maximum level of £9,000 fees per annum for undergraduate degree programmes. In doing so, the Coalition government more firmly established in England what was already an already emerging competitive market in HE: not a free market, but a market which the government manipulates through student numbers controls, the system of loans and the introduction of private providers. These measures have all introduced new levels of complexity that are throwing up interesting paradoxes: counter-intuitive paradoxes, such as the fact that the trebling of fees has not affected recruitment overall from traditional applicants to full-time degree programmes and the sort of paradox illustrated in the following two headlines:

> UCAS: top universities should consider BTEC students.
>
> (Telegraph, 2014)

> Tens of thousands of teenagers are denying themselves the opportunity of studying at the top universities by taking vocational courses in the sixth-form or at college.
>
> (Sutton Trust, 2013)

These headlines refer to the concern that the chief executive of the Universities and Colleges Admissions Service (UCAS) expressed about the declining number of traditional A-level candidates and the rising number of Business and Technician Education Council (BTEC) candidates. Put together, the headlines illustrate a paradox between structure and agency – the first argues for structural change within 'top' universities to take account of vocational qualifications or face 'restrict(ed) recruitment' in the future. The second headline focuses on individual agency, placing on vocational students themselves the burden that they are disadvantaging themselves by taking vocational courses that will not get them into 'top' universities. The real paradox here resides in the commonly expressed but potentially flawed assumption that these vocational students necessarily want to apply to 'top universities' and that they necessarily have the same aspirations and ambitions as 'traditional', or 'top' A-level, students.

Commentators and politicians whose own experiences are based on public schools, grammar school or 'top' comprehensive education followed by a Russell Group university may, arguably, perceive that the norm for a student pathway across the educational landscape comprises a relatively straight, well signposted progression journey from elite school through to first-class university. Coffield observes of the sector in relation to commentators external to it: "this fascinating, turbulent, insecure but desperately important world . . . remains invisible to most politicians, academics and commentators because, with very few exceptions, neither they nor their children have ever passed through it" (Coffield, 2006: 2). This paper argues, by contrast, that the 'norm' for a significant number of students in England is rather different from this kind of often assumed easy progression route.

New research (Joslin & Smith, 2013; Joslin & Smith, 2014; Joslin *et al.*, 2015a, 2015b and 2015c) into the longitudinal progression routes of non-traditional vocational students, including the progression pathways of apprentices, can help to place some new, more meaningful small markers in a chaotic educational landscape that seems otherwise almost impossible to understand and navigate at the whole system level. These additional markers contribute in significant ways to update existing knowledge of HE progression in England, joining some of the dots of individual pathways to make more sense of students' often complex, alternative journeys to HE.

Prior research on progression to HE has previously highlighted the disparity in HE progression between learners studying, for example traditional A-level qualifications who progress at a rate of around 90 per cent (Carter, 2009) compared with BTEC learners (HEFCE, 2007), of whom 41 per cent progressed based on a longitudinal analysis of the 2002–03 cohort. New research on the progression of FE learners from all the colleges of FE and sixth form colleges in England provides an update to these findings (Smith *et al.*, 2015a). This research tracked over 1.8 million level-three FE students over five years (2007–08 to 2011–12). Of these, 40 per cent were found to have come from the most disadvantaged neighbourhoods in England. When tracked over a number of years, 48 per cent of these FE and sixth form college students progressed to higher education. For these college students, progression rates depended on the qualifications they took and the period during which they studied: around 42 per cent of BTEC students progressed until 2012 entry when fees rose and the figure dropped to 30 per cent. This is compared to around 68 per cent of A-level/IB students progressing until 2012 entry, when the figure dropped to 61 per cent. Latterly, however, an increase in BTEC entrants to HE has also been more widely reported from elsewhere in England. In 2012, UCAS announced UCAS/Department for Education government proposals to reform vocational qualifications for 16–19-year-olds, stating that BTECs are now the second most widely used HE entry qualification and that the proportion of students entering HE with purely academic qualifications had fallen from 70 per cent in 2008 to 51 per cent in 2012, which is further evidence of the increasing currency of vocational qualifications for HE entry.

Prior research on the progression of apprentices to HE quoted a progression rate of 6 per cent (UKCES, 2010). This was based on a HEFCE report in the series "Pathways to Higher Education" on apprentices (HEFCE, 2009). The most recent report in the BIS Research Report series "Progression of Apprentices to Higher Education" (Smith *et al.*, 2015b) finds that, when tracked longitudinally into higher education over seven years, the progression rate is 19.3 per cent. This is indeed a larger figure, but it does not come close to the aspirational statistic given by the National Apprenticeship Service of 50 per cent of advanced level apprentices showing "interest in pursuing a degree-level equivalent course" (NAS, 2011) or the 54 per cent figure of apprentices in London who said that it was "very likely that they would undertake further training or learning leading to a qualification within 2 to 3 years of finishing their course" (IFF Research, 2012).

The new research findings reported here on the progression of vocational learners into HE is based on a methodology of matching level 3 FE learners and advanced level apprentice cohorts from ILR datasets with level 4 learners non-prescribed HE or higher apprenticeship ILR datasets with HESA data covering all prescribed HE. Each cohort is matched for each year of entry so that for the latest apprentice study, the data obtained is found in Figure 4.2 (Smith *et al.*, 2015b).

Advanced level apprentice cohort start year	Population	Number 2006-07	2007-08	2008-09	2009-10	2010-11	2011-12	2012-13	HE immediate progression (3 years tracking)	% HE progression	Total number to HE (All tracked to date)	% HE progression	Number of years tracked
2006-07	34870	420	1325	2145	1040	835	590	370	3890	11.2%	6725	19.3%	7 yrs
2007-08	40785		495	1850	2430	1130	825	560	4775	11.7%	7290	17.9%	6 yrs
2008-09	49215			1110	2095	2610	1235	775	5815	11.8%	7820	15.9%	5 yrs
2009-10	57475				1300	2430	2540	1155	6275	10.9%	7430	12.9%	4 yrs
2010-11	62110					1110	2735	1610	5450	8.8%	5450	8.8%	3 yrs
2011-12	13925*						515	710	na	na	1225	8.8%	2 yrs
Total	244455	420	1820	5105	6865	8115	8440	5180	26205		35940		

Figure 4.2 Advanced level apprenticeships progression in England 2006–07 to 2012–13

* NB – It takes most advanced level apprentices up to two years to complete their framework, so this population does not include those who started in 2011 but had not yet completed their framework when the data was linked. The cohort populations will change in updates as apprentices who complete their framework are included in the tracking study.

What the data in Figure 4.2 tell us is that the progression journeys of apprentices are much more complex than those of full-time A-level and other students. Many of them enter HE in the same academic year as they complete their apprenticeships, and this is partly explained by the fact that about 50 per cent of advanced level apprentices have already studied at this level (BIS, 2011). Thereafter, there are significant numbers who progress one or two years later and still relatively high figures who progress three, four, five and six years after that. The reasons for these patterns of progression are manifold. They relate to the overriding fact that these are part-time learners in work, often with good jobs, who, if they are looking to progress, will look for further part-time provision; they relate to the fact that these learners might not have the entry requirements necessary for HE entry (Fuller & Unwin, 2012); they also relate to the fact that these are journeys made by people who have real lives, who are perhaps gaining more responsibility at work, may be having children, moving home, losing their jobs, changing career direction.

So what are the key factors involved in determining which apprentices make the journey to higher education? This chapter explores three key factors, highlighting what the research findings are and signposting where further exploration needs to take place.

A first important factor picked up in the apprenticeship research is that, over the five cohort years 2006–07 and 2011–12, there has been a steady fall in progression to college-delivered HE from 63 per cent in 2006–07 to 52 per cent in 2010–11 with a consequent rise in numbers progressing to universities. One explanation for this trend lies in what has been described as conflicting policy moves by the two (then) key funding agencies, the Learning and Skills Council (LSC) and HEFCE (Parry *et al.*, 2012), and how, during the timescales covered by this research on apprentice progression, Higher National Diplomas (HNDs) and Higher National Certificates (HNCs), previously the dominant HE offer in FE colleges, were being "eclipsed" by the expansion of Foundation degrees. A surprising aspect of the move away from FE-delivered HE provision for these students is that in 2006–07, 68.4 per cent of them went on to continue to study part time. By 2010–11, this had fallen away to 50.3 per cent. This is surprising because FE colleges are set up to provide locally accessible part-time provision and have very good links with their local employers, including those who have advanced apprentices. With some exceptions, notably the Open University and Birkbeck, University of London, universities are not set up to provide off-the-job training in the same way as colleges with block release, evening courses and part-time twilight provision to fit around the needs of people in work. Colleges are also able to access funding for non-prescribed HE for programmes such as NVQs and professional courses. More needs to be known about the reasons why colleges have not actively promoted their part-time HE provision, but it is probably more a question of a lack of strategic thinking about this area of work during a period when they have been buffeted year on year with funding changes that have forced a focus away from adult provision to full-time provision to the 16–19 age group. Although we do not have the full figures yet for apprentice progression over the years 2011 and 2012, which saw a real drop in part-time HE numbers, with the exception of earlier work on part-time HE (Pollard et al., 2012), subsequent research (HEFCE, 2014; Oxford Economics, 2014; Universities UK, 2013) does not focus on apprentices, which are a rapidly growing constituency of part-time students. Could one of the causes of the lowering progression rate of apprentices be a lack of local supply of flexible part-time HE (see for example Fuller & Unwin, 2014)? If it is, might higher apprenticeships be able to fill the gap or should higher nationals be reset so that the HNC is re-established as the dominant part-time qualification offered by colleges following a strategic review of local employer needs?

A second key factor the research reveals is that there has been a fall in the overall in-year or immediate progression "rate" when like-for-like three-year progression periods are compared. Over the five cohorts, the immediate progression rate has dropped from 11.2 per cent for the 2006–07 cohort to 8.8 per cent for the 2010–11 cohort. Figure 4.2 shows that while the rate has been dropping, the overall numbers progressing have been increasing, as have the numbers of advanced level apprentices, by a figure of 27,240 over the five years between 2006–07 and 2010–11.

To explain the reason for the fall in the rate of this immediate progression, it is necessary first to look at the age profile of the cohort where much of the increase in advanced apprentice numbers was people aged over 25. Next, it is revealing to look at the gender profile which shows that the majority of the growth was an increase in the numbers of female apprentices over 25. Between 2006–07 and 2010–11 the number of female apprentices doubled from 14,145 to 35,475. What lies behind this large increase in female advanced apprentices and especially from those over 25? Recent evaluations of apprenticeship provision from both the apprentice and employer perspective throw some light on this (Ipsos MORI, 2014a, 2014b). In interviews with apprentices, the data shows that it is those in the more traditional apprenticeships such as engineering and construction, as well as social care, public services and health who are more likely to view their apprenticeship as a route to a career. Their employers in these sectors were also more likely to offer a further qualification, including higher apprenticeships, HNCs, Foundation degrees and Honours degrees. But, as the Ipsos MORI report says,

> The recent expansion in Apprenticeship numbers has been in newer, less traditional frameworks dominated by three framework groups in particular: *Business, Administration and Law* (157% growth in starts between 2008/09 and 2011/12); *Health and Public Services* (214% growth in starts); and *Retail and Commercial Enterprise* (125% growth in starts). These frameworks groups are also associated with the least amount, and shortest duration, of training.
>
> (Ipsos MORI, 2014a: 7)

These also happen to be frameworks where females aged 25+ dominate and, as such apprentices are less 'career oriented', there is much less expectation among employers and apprentices about progression to higher education. The 'expansive-restrictive' apprenticeship continuum sheds light on these different sorts of advanced apprenticeship, while other limiting factors in addition to qualification pervade the culture of some apprenticeship frameworks (Fuller & Unwin, 2011).

Finally, the third key factor relates to who else these 'non-traditional' HE students are, where they come from and how different their social backgrounds are from those of 'traditional' HE entrants. Since anonymised individual data about the learners is available when matching the aforementioned databases, we are able to relate postcodes to the various indices of deprivation. For the apprenticeship research, HEFCE's Participation of Local Areas (POLAR) classifications have been used, showing areas with differing take-up of HE. POLAR quintiles 1 and 2 represent domiciles with the lowest take-up of HE, and it is generally reckoned that this is a good proxy for deprivation (HEFCE, 2012).

Significantly, around 22 per cent of apprentices who progress to HE come from POLAR quintiles 1 and 2, compared with 11 per cent of all young undergraduate entrants and 12 per cent for mature undergraduate entrants (HEFCE, 2012). This suggests that apprenticeships provide a platform for social mobility, but a deeper look at the data shows that this is the case for certain frameworks (engineering, accountancy, business administration, health and social care, sporting excellence, dental nursing and IT services and development) but not necessarily for others (Joslin & Smith, 2014: 57). Age and gender also play into this analysis, and there are regional variations as well.

If apprenticeships lead to social mobility and improved progression across multiple pathways, as the data suggest, more detailed analysis needs to be undertaken to understand the influences of and interrelationships between age, domicile, framework, qualification, gender, and local and regional supply of appropriate HE. The identification of such patterns based on longitudinal individual learner records will enable new forms of sense-making at multiple levels across the complex post-compulsory education landscape.

Conclusion

This paper begins to connect the dots in the discovery and systematic detailed mapping of new data on longitudinal progression routes taken by vocational students in FE and apprenticeships provision into HE in England at both a mass and individual level. The paper aims to contribute to new forms of sense-making (Weick, 2012) and a reduction in confusion about learner progression routes, enabling also the potential development of an improved ecosystem and more trusted educational environment at the individual learner level in post-compulsory education in the longer term.

The supercomplexity of the existing FE and apprenticeships landscape in England has obscured data collection and analysis hitherto, as no agency has previously been able to carry out accurate large-scale national mapping from one system to another to measure individual student longitudinal FE-apprenticeships-HE progression pathways in England. The team at Greenwich is working on the development of the methodology, tracking system and data analysis resulting from this ground-breaking research and will continue to report on the analysis of the progression datasets over the next few years. This chapter therefore provides an initial report from a larger set of publications still emerging.

The aim overall is to reduce the level of bewildering complexity in the further and post-compulsory education sector so that students' actual progression pathways are more easily known and understood. The sense-making aspects of this at a systemic level may contribute to the formation of more detailed evidence-informed policy making, research, institutional management and professional practice. Ultimately, the detailed, accurate longitudinal tracking and measurement of individual learner progress from FE and apprenticeships to HE could theoretically result in an improved landscape in which policy makers, managers and teachers could build on progression dataset feedback to improve provision at local, regional and national levels.

The potential for vastly improved, accurate destination data could result in a wide range of longer-term benefits. These could include positive impacts on local institutional governing body and senior management strategic planning through to student support services and curriculum delivery. In envisaging the potential for this, the research team recognises the need to report with both sufficient clarity and also detailed local specificity to enable progression pathways to be accurately mapped in a complex landscape. As Albert Einstein once said, "Everything should be made as simple as possible, but not simpler" (Silk, 2011).

References

Barnett, R. (2000) *Realizing the University in an Age of Supercomplexity*. Milton Keynes: Open University Press.

BIS. (2011) *Prior Qualifications of Adult Apprentices 2009–10*. London: BIS.

Caiden, G.E. (1985) Excessive bureaucratization: The J-curve theory of bureaucracy and Max Weber through the looking glass. *Dialogue*, 7(4), 21–33. http://www.jstor.org/stable/25610452 (Accessed 18 February 2016)

Carter, P. J. (2009). *Progression from Vocational and Applied Learning to Higher Education in England*. University Vocational Awards Council (UVAC).

Coffield, F. (2006) *Running Ever Faster Down The Wrong Road: An Alternative Future For Education and Skills*. Inaugural Lecture at the Institute of Education, 5th December, 2006. London, England: Institute of Education, University of London. https://www.researchgate.net/profile/Frank_Coffield/publication/265869845_Running_Ever_Faster_Down_the_Wrong_Road_An_Alternative_Future_for_Education_and_Skills/links/54e0b0fa0cf24d184b0bdb61.pdf (Accessed 31 May 2016)

Evans, K., Waite, E. and Kersh, N. (2011) Towards a social ecology of adult learning in and through the workplace, in M. Malloch, L. Cairns, K. Evans and B. N. O'Connor (eds.) *The SAGE Handbook of Workplace Learning*. London: Sage, pp. 356–70.

Fuller, A. and Unwin, L. (2011) The content of apprenticeships, in T. Dolphin and T. Lanning (eds.) *Rethinking Apprenticeships*. London: IPPR, pp. 29–39.

Fuller, A. and Unwin, L. (2012) *Banging on the Doors of the University: The Complexities of Progression from Apprenticeship and Other Vocational Preogrammes in England.* Cardiff: SKOPE.
Fuller, A. and Unwin, L. (2014) *Apprenticeship and the Concept of Occupation.* London: The Gatsby Charitable Foundation. http://www.gatsby.org.uk/~/media/Files/Education/Apprenticeship%20and%20the%20Concept%20of%20Occupation.ashx (Accessed February 2016)
HEFCE. (2007) *Pathways to Higher Education – BTEC Courses.* Bristol: HEFCE.
HEFCE. (2009) *Pathways to Higher Education – Apprenticeships.* Bristol: HEFCE.
HEFCE. (2012) *POLAR 3 Young Participation in Higher Education.* Bristol: HEFCE.
HEFCE. (2014) *Pressure from All Sides – Economic and Policy Influences on Part-Time Higher Education.* Bristol: HEFCE.
Hillier, Y. and Jameson, J. (2003) *Empowering Researchers in Further Education.* Stoke on Trent: Trentham Books.
IFF Research. (2012) *Evaluation of Apprenticeships: London Region Findings.* London: BIS.
The Innovation, Universities, Science and Skills Committee, House of Commons. (2008) *Re-skilling for Recovery: After Leitch, Implementing Skills and Training Policies.* London: The Stationery Office.
Ipsos MORI. (2014a) *Apprenticehip Evaluation: Learners.* London: BIS.
Ipsos MORI. (2014b) *Apprenticeships Evaluation: Employers.* London: BIS.
Jameson, J. (2006) *Leadership in Post-Compulsory Education: Inspiring Leaders of the Future.* London: David Fulton/Routledge Publishers.
Jameson, J. (2007) Series Foreword and Introduction, Essential FE Toolkit Series, in C. Winch and T. Hyland (eds.) *A Guide to Vocational Education and Training.* London: Bloomsbury Academic, pp. vii–xii.
Jameson, J. and Hillier, Y. (2003) *Researching Post-Compulsory Education.* Continuum Research Methods Series. London: Continuum.
Jameson, J. and Hillier, Y. (2008) 'Nothing will prevent me from doing a good job': The professionalisation of part-time teaching staff in further and adult education. *Research in Postcompulsory Education,* 13(1), 39–53.
Joslin, H. and Smith, S. (2013) *Progression of College Learners to Higher Education in London.* London: Linking London.
Joslin, H. and Smith, S. (2014) *Progression of Apprentices to Higher Education – Cohort Update.* London: Department for Business, Innovation and Skills (BIS).
Karr, J.B.A. (1849) January Edition of Les Guêpes, p. vi.
NAO. (2011) *Re-Skilling for Recovery: After Leitch, Implementing Skills and Training Policies.* London: The Stationery Office.
NAS. (2011) *Higher Apprenticeship Fund Prospectus.* National Apprenticeship Service.
Oxford Economics. (2014) *Macroeconomic Influences on the Demand for Part-time Higher Education in the UK.* Oxford: Oxford Economics.
Parry, G., Callender, C., Scott, P. and Temple, P. (2012) *Understanding Higher Education in Further Education Colleges.* BIS.
Parry, G. and Thompson, A. (2002) *Closer by Degrees: The Past, Present and Future of Higher Education in Further Education Colleges.* LSDA Research Report No. R1164. London: Learning and Skills Development Agency.
Pollard, E., Newton, B. and Hillage, J. (2012) *Expanding and Improving Part-time Higher Education.* BIS.

Policy Consortium. (2014) *Taking the Pulse of Further Education: The Great FE and Skills Survey of 2014.* Report produced with FE Week. London: Policy Consortium. http://goo.gl/BgtYUO (Accessed February 2016)

Solman, G. (1993) The passion of Bill Murray. *Film Comment,* 29(6), 5.

Sherlock, D. and Perry, N. (2013) *Further Education in 2020: Making the System Work.* 157 Group Report. London: 157 Group. http://goo.gl/hmNsk8 (Accessed February 2016)

Silk, J. (2011) *Horizons of Cosmology.* West Conshohocken, PA: Templeton Press.

Smith, S., Joslin, H. and Jameson, J. (2015a) *Progression of College Students in England to Higher Education.* BIS Research Paper Number 239. London: Department for Business, Innovation and Skills (BIS). https://goo.gl/KF5gAh (Accessed February 2016)

Smith, S., Joslin, H. and Jameson, J. (2015b) *Progression of College Students in London to Higher Education, 2007 to 2012.* London: Linking London. http://www.london councils.gov.uk/node/27630 (Accessed February 2016)

Smith, S., Joslin, H. and Jameson, J. (2015c) *Progression of Apprentices to Higher Education: 2nd Cohort Update.* BIS Research Paper Number 240. London: Linking London, BIS. https://goo.gl/JZYv7L (Accessed February 2016)

Sutton Trust. (2013) *John O'Leary Blog Post: The Vocational Challenge.* http://www.sutt ontrust.com/news/blog/advancing-access-blog-four/ (Accessed November 2013)

Telegraph. (2014) *Graeme Paton, Education Editor.* UCAS: Top Universities should Consider BTEC Students. http://goo.gl/2AFjTZ (Accessed 30 April 2014)

UKCES. (2010) *Progression from Vocational and Applied Learning to Higher Education Across the UK.* UK Commission for Employment and Skills.

Universities UK. (2013) *The Power of Part-time – Review of Part-Time and Mature Higher Education.* London: Universities UK.

Weick, K. E. (2012) Organized sensemaking: A commentary on processes of interpretive work. *Human Relations,* 65(1), 141–153.

Whittaker, F. (2014) News. http://feweek.co.uk/2014/04/24/huge-survey-lifts-lid-on-sector/ (Accessed 24 April 2014)

Winch, C. and Hyland, T. (2007) *A Guide to Vocational Education and Training.* London: Bloomsbury Academic, Series Ed. J. Jameson, The Essential FE Toolkit Series.

Section 2
Programmes

5 A question of identity
Does it do what it says on the tin?

Prue Huddleston

Background

Since the 1944 Education Act, and even before, continuous attempts have been made to provide an appropriate curriculum for young people beyond 14 years of age who wish to pursue a vocational pathway. Many of these attempts have resulted in disappointment for learners and employers, dilution of strong vocational content and learning and even downright disaster in some cases.

This chapter aims to review some of the evidence to date about why the design and delivery of strong and credible vocational programmes for post-14 learners has been so challenging and what this means for young people who are now required to remain in some form of education and training beyond 16 (DfES, 2007; DfE, 2012). How can they be assured that what they are offered fulfils the claims on the label?

Attempts to provide vocational 'qualifications', 'programmes', 'routes', 'pathways' (call them what you will, although they are not the same thing, and herein lies part of the problem) for this age group have occupied policy makers for the past 30 years at least (Stanton, 2006; Stanton & Bailey, 2005). Some of them, often quite excellent programmes, such as Unified Vocational Preparation and Certificate of Pre-Vocational Education (CPVE), disappeared, others underwent several adaptations, for example the General National Vocational Qualification (GNVQ) and the Advanced Vocational Certificate of Education (AVCE) before finally 'morphing' into quasi-academic qualifications, while others have stood the test of time, for example BTECs and City and Guilds qualifications.

The provision of technical and vocational education was once the monopoly of technical colleges and colleges of further education, outside that provided by employers within workplaces, for young people post-16. However, for the past two decades, schools have become significant providers of so-called vocational programmes, initially for post-16 students but more recently for pre-16 students as well. This led to the now famous 'perverse incentives' described by Wolf (Wolf, 2011), the 'four for the price of one' culture, with schools attempting to boost 'league table' scores by entering students for numbers of so-called vocational qualifications with spurious equivalence to general qualifications and little connection to any occupational sector.

The introduction of the Diplomas in 2008 represented another attempt to nail the problem, but they also perished before full implementation was achieved

(Ertl & Stasz, 2010; Huddleston & Laczik, 2012). The Raising of the Participation Age (RPA) to 17 from summer 2013 and to 18 by summer 2015 has posed the question yet again: what type of provision should be made available for those who perforce are required to remain in some form of education and training to 18? (Acquah & Huddleston, 2014; Simmons, 2008).

What is clear is that something more than standard academic fare, or poor quality 'make-weight' courses, have to be offered. The question as to what this offering should be has proved elusive for policy makers, not least because this provision is often referred to as 'vocational' without any clear understanding, or shared agreement, about what is meant by 'vocational'. In the case of the 'doomed' Diplomas, for example (QCA, 2006) this nomenclature proved even more challenging. During the period of their development (2005–07) they were variously described as 'specialist vocational Diplomas' (Lord Adonis), 'betwixt the academic and the vocational' (schools minister), 'not vocational in one sense, but they are in another' (secretary of state), 'applied Diplomas', 'integrated Diplomas', 'specialised Diplomas' and, finally, just plain 'Diplomas' (House of Commons, 2007). The rest is silence.

Old problems, new contexts

One of the major challenges inherent in the 16–19 reform proposals is that there are a number of policy drivers – economic, social and technological – some of which may be in tension. It could be argued that education and training reform is a blunt instrument with which to tackle the multi-headed Hydra of 'low participation', 'low productivity', 'global competitiveness', 'low levels of attainment', 'disengagement', 'youth unemployment' and 'an ageing population' – to list but a few of the challenges allegedly besetting the system. The result of this conflation, if not confusion, of purposes is often to label things incorrectly, almost as a kind of shorthand. This is nowhere more apparent than in the use of the term 'vocational' to describe qualifications, programmes and courses which are clearly not vocational in the fullest sense of the word, but are not academic programmes either.

Two problems immediately arise. First, there is a tendency to lump together everything which appears not to be an 'academic' subject as vocational, although it can be argued that all subjects can have a vocational application. It would be unlikely for anyone to achieve a qualification in engineering without having the necessary knowledge and understanding of the underpinning mathematics. Nowhere has this situation been starker than for those young people who wished to remain in some form of education beyond 16 but who had insufficient 'academic' passes at an acceptable standard to do so. They were perforce navigated towards so-called 'vocational' provision with little understanding of what this might entail and where it might lead (Huddleston, 2002). Much of this provision was not vocational at all, in that it was not delivered by vocational specialists, it did not include exposure to industry-standard equipment or practices and it did not include access to relevant workplaces. Often it also failed to provide suitable opportunities for progression.

Second, 'vocational' becomes associated with a view that it is "a way of dealing with the disadvantaged and disaffected rather than a high quality route to gaining technical or managerial-level skills, this could have negative implications for their status" (Stasz & Wright, 2004: 27). In a darker vein, during a recent visit to a secondary school to interview young people participating in a school-college link programme, the author was told that one teacher referred to the transport used to take students from school to college as 'the prison ships'.

Since the publication of the *Review of Vocational Qualifications – The Wolf Report* (Wolf, 2011) – these issues have re-emerged within the context of the proposed 16–19 Study Programmes (DfE, 2015). If young people are being forced to engage in some form of education and training post-16, what exactly will be the offer? Clearly, the majority of these 'new' learners will not be following the 'royal route' of A-levels. Nor will they be following a fully work-based apprenticeship route. Social equity dictates that they should have access to high-quality education and training, wherever it is delivered, and that such provision should allow progression to FE, training or employment.

In a speech delivered at the Sunday Times Festival of Education in 2014, Matthew Hancock (then minister for skills) tried to 'see off' the association with 'routes of no return' by stating that,

> We've scrapped the confusion of different pathways, at 14, 16, and beyond – and brought in a new, rigorous, ambitious vocational offer from 14 right through to 19 and beyond.
> (Matthew Hancock, speech to the Sunday Times Festival of Education, Wellington College, June 2014)

The use of the term 'vocational' is significant here since it suggests, yet again, that everything that is not an A-level will be vocational. If this is the intention, how do the proposals for the 16–19 Study Programmes match the expectations of truly vocational programmes?

The prescription

Study Programmes are guided by a 'set of principles' (DfE, 2015) that *'all students 16–19,* "whether doing academic or vocational studies, or a mix of both, are expected to follow a programme of study tailored to their prior attainment by age 16 and future education and career aspirations" (p.5). The rationale underpinning Study Programmes and the criteria against which Ofsted will make judgments are that they

- Provide progression to a higher level than prior attainment
- Include qualifications that are of sufficient size to provide 'stretch and rigour' and allow progression into FE, training or employment
- Require students who have not already attained an A*–C grade in maths and English to work towards them, or to other approved English or maths qualifications at the same level

- Include work experience – linked to study programme, to develop employability skills, or to create employment options for those unable to follow a 'substantial' vocational qualification
- Include other activities, non-qualification, to develop 'character', 'skills' 'attitudes' and 'confidence'

(Adapted from DfE, 2015: 5)

For well over a decade, similar goals have been widely expressed in both international and national policy documents on qualifications, including the former Diplomas in England – namely that qualifications should

- be transparent in terms of what they signify and what must be achieved
- minimise barriers to progression both vertical and horizontal
- maximise access, flexibility and portability between different sectors of education and work and different sites of learning

(Young, 2003: 224)

Table 5.1 provides characteristics of the 16–19 Study Programmes.

Table 5.1 Characteristics of 16–19 study programmes

Substantial qualification(s)	*English and maths*	*Work experience*	*Other activities*
A-levels *or* Tech level qualifications (level 3) *or* Applied General qualifications (level 3) *or* Technical certificates (level 2) *(possibility of mixing qualifications but to a limited extent)*	Students who do not hold GCSE A*–C must be enrolled on a GCSE. Students already holding GCSE maths should be encouraged to study a level 3 maths qualification (e.g. core maths). Students following Traineeships and Supported provision should study English and maths at a level suited to their prior attainment and progression goals.	Should be provided for all students with an external employer and in a workplace environment. Students not taking a substantial vocational qualification, those on Traineeships and Supported internships, should spend the majority of their time on work experience and developing employability skills.	Non-qualification activity, for example volunteering, Duke of Edinburgh Award, work to develop employability skills.
Other provision			
Traineeships (should not last more than six months). Supported internships (for those with learning difficulties and disabilities).			

A question of identity 57

Whilst the former minister described Study Programmes as a "new, rigorous, ambitious vocational offer from 14 right through to 19 and beyond", a glance at the first column in Table 5.1 indicates several qualifications that will comprise the substantial element of Study Programmes: A-levels, Tech levels, Applied General qualifications and Technical certificates. For those not yet ready to embark on 'substantial' level 2 qualifications, there are other options – namely, Traineeships or Supported Internships. It is clear that these are not all vocational qualifications, for example several titles are in use – Tech level, Technical certificate, Applied General qualification. A-level is self-evident. At the same time, all students are expected to have some exposure to workplaces and to develop employability skills (columns three and four in Table 5.1). The opportunities for confusion are multiple: for example what is distinctive about technical as opposed to applied? What is the purpose of work experience within the different programmes (learning for work, about work or at work)? What do 'employability skills' mean within the context of these programmes?

A further reflection may be offered, that is a realisation that some of these qualifications should not be regarded as truly vocational but that they are general qualifications set within a broad vocational context. The Applied General qualifications, currently under development, appear to fall into this category.

> Applied General qualifications are level 3 (advanced) qualifications that provide broad study of a vocational area. They are recognised by at least three Higher Education Institutions (HEIs) as fulfilling entry requirements to a range of HE courses, either in their own right or alongside other level 3 qualifications. Some employers and professional/trade bodies have also pledged support for Applied General qualifications.
>
> (DfE, 2014: 3)

In submitting these qualifications for approval to the Office of Qualifications and Examinations Regulation (Ofqual), awarding organisations are required to append letters of endorsement from HEIs and, in some cases, employers, although for Applied General qualifications, employer endorsement in not mandatory. However, for Tech levels and Technical certificates, endorsement by employers (up to eight) is a requirement. Similarly, the content is expected to reflect the needs of the sector and to mirror workplace practice in the setting and performance of assessment tasks:

> It is aimed at 16–18 Year old learners who are seeking to develop skills in marketing for entry into this sector" (extract from AQA specification Tech level Business Marketing). This awarding organisation also states that in developing Tech levels it has: "worked with employers and professional bodies to design, structure and concept test our Tech levels. They help fill a workplace skills gap identified by employers and CBI surveys, and respond to government reform.
>
> (AQA: DfE, 2014: 3)

Working with employers on qualification design does not automatically assure that the delivery of such qualifications will meet criteria for strong vocational programmes – namely that they are set within realistic work contexts, reflect current workplace practice, are resourced by appropriately qualified and experienced staff and deploy up-to-date skills, techniques and equipment relevant to the sector.

Such distinctions are important and have not been made sufficiently clear in the past, thus leading to confusion about the purposes and possible outcomes of qualifications. This confusion of purposes leads to differing expectations from learners and, it has to be said, employers. If a young person signs up to a qualification designated 'engineering design' or 'beauty therapy', it would be reasonable to assume that the programme would include practical 'hands on' experience of the sector both in terms of the resources available and the context in which it is located. Young people should not be 'sold' such qualifications on the basis of their portability and credibility in the workplace if this is not the case. Research has shown that this was frequently a problem in the precursor GNVQ (Intermediate) qualifications (Huddleston, 2002, DfE, 2014: 3.)

Employers may be under the impression that someone leaving such programmes is 'work ready'; in other words, they are expecting someone with a level of occupational competence appropriate for the tasks that they might be asked to perform in the workplace. The confusion of expectation arises because the employer is seeking occupational competence, whilst the young person has been pursuing a programme not designed to achieve occupational competence but to provide a broad introduction to a vocational area. Unless these differing purposes are made clear, both parties are labouring under a false impression. It might be proposed that the type of programme being suggested by many of the so-called vocational routes is preparatory rather than full-blown vocational education. This may well prove to be the case in the new Applied General qualifications currently under development.

It is reasonable to expect that all full-time programmes for young people 16–19, whatever label we might wish to give them, should provide opportunities for the integration of general education with wider developmental opportunities, for example personal learning and thinking skills, as well as the opportunity to pursue individual interests in the form of extended studies, projects or activities. The unfortunate reality is that so often these are set out as desirable only for those who have been designated as 'needy' in some way, or who have been steered towards a 'vocational' route. As a result, the vocational takes on the mantle of a 'compensatory' programme, not a programme in its own right. Previous attempts to offer 'life skills', 'core skills', 'employability skills' and 'functional skills' within vocational programmes met with varying degrees of success, often as a result of poor integration and contextualisation within the main area of study. Yet, at the same time, employers have consistently argued the need to develop such skills (CBI, 2014; Felstead *et al.*, 2002; Huddleston & Fettes, 2000; Le Métais, 2002; UKCES, 2014).

In this latest prescription, all students are expected to have access to an integrated programme, as outlined in Table 5.1. However, those not working at level 2 are to 'spend the majority of their time on work experience and developing employability skills'. The detail of this remains unspecified and it is left up to schools and colleges to make of it what they can. At the same time, those following Tech levels and Technical certificates are expected to have access to workplaces and to realistic learning environments. Their curriculum is to be informed by employer inputs. It is not clear how all this can be achieved within the budgetary constraints placed upon the education sector, in particular those placed on FE (Skills Commission, 2015).

Early responses to the implementation of 16–19 Study Programmes (AOC, 2014; Ofsted, 2014) suggest that the provision of work experience on this scale will be extremely difficult to achieve and that colleges lack the capacity to deliver the maths and English requirements for all students. Similarly, links with employers were found to be patchy. It is yet to be seen how far the Study Programmes will provide an integrated learning experience for all students, as suggested in the 'set of principles' or if the default position will pertain. In other words, it could be better for some than for others.

In outlining its initial proposals for raising of the participation age to 18, the Department for Education and Skills (DfES) (2007) recognised the need to have an 'engaging curriculum in place' for all learners. As Lord (2006) suggests,

> Young people need to see the point of it all. They especially want practical application (not just practical work). This might be learning about a job, developing personal skills, experiencing team work or having a subject explained to them in terms of its contemporary context.
>
> (p. 2)

Or as a young person recently reported: "I do not need to do harder maths if I want to be a graphic designer, or a hairdresser. I need to do practical things better".

It is too early to say if the new proposals will assure this.

Qualifications, qualifications, qualifications

The current obsession with qualifications, as the only metric of achievement, results in every proposed reform of vocational education and training being expressed in terms of a new qualification, or suites of qualifications. In the discussion so far, it will have been noted that the reforms proposed within the new 16–19 Study Programmes are presented mainly in terms of new, or revised, qualifications, which indeed they are, but that is not the whole story. The 16–19 'set of principles' are predicated upon much broader reform, for example the need to provide a wider curriculum offer that includes opportunities for 'enrichment' activities (see Table 5.1, column 4), the desire for the study of maths and English to be integrated into all students' learning (see Table 5.1, column 2). Stanton (2004) has persuasively argued that "vocational programmes may better meet the needs of many learners as much because of their integrated structure as their vocational content." (p.5). To focus predominantly on the content of the qualification in terms of the Tech level, Technical certificate and Applied General design rather than on the implications for wider curriculum opportunities, pedagogy, staff development and resourcing, including effective partnerships with employers, is to forgo the possibility of providing a truly integrated offer.

In designing the new Study Programmes for 16–19 year olds, the qualifications and their associated assessment and grading regimes, academic drift has already set in. This is characterised by an emphasis on terminal externally marked tests and examinations, fewer re-sit opportunities, greater emphasis on theoretical knowledge and less on practical application and performance. Strong justification is required for the use of internal assessment. However, there is no clear guidance on, or expectation of, how the other elements of Study Programmes are to be met. For example what will count as enrichment activity? What quality criteria should pertain in work experience? How are these elements to link with the qualification being taken? Is there a danger that the 16–19 Study Programmes will be, yet again, more about new qualifications than about strong vocational programmes?

Successful vocational programmes are truly integrative, bringing together a number of elements which enable a learner to see the vocational area, and his or her place within it, as a coherent whole. Vocational programmes should only be described as such if a certain number of conditions are in place. Namely that those who teach on such programmes are "experienced in the occupation or workplace concerned; can themselves perform to work-place standards; and have access to industry-standard facilities and equipment" (Stanton, 2006). The young people following such programmes must be allowed access to real learning environments where the practical experience will help to consolidate and reinforce learning which takes place in the classroom or workshops. Schools and/or colleges which cannot guarantee this provision should not be allowed to deliver Tech levels or Technical certificates. Similarly, as currently specified, Applied General qualifications should not be presented, or offered, as full-blown vocational qualifications.

The purpose

This sense of 'wholeness' includes within it notions of identity. When trainee chefs put on kitchen 'whites' and buy their first set of knives, they cross the boundary from passive student to active participant in a community of practice (Lave & Wenger, 1991; Tuomi-Grohn & Engrestrom, 2003). Some identities may be easier to embrace than others, but part of the identity formation involves proximity to 'real' practitioners. At its most extreme, this may be expressed in terms of 'I trained with . . .' as if the invocation of the famed practitioner were sufficient to guarantee outstanding talent in the trainee. In terms of what has been proposed previously, and currently, within vocational qualifications reform, it might be suggested that the only role model that school teachers provide is that of teacher. In the case of college staff, they frequently possess a dual professionalism: teacher and craftsperson, for example.

> Teachers of vocational pathways in schools are not required to have experience of, or expertise of, the vocational pathway. This is not acceptable in further education and should not be the case in schools.
> (Skills Commission, undated: 9)

Contexts carry powerful connotations in terms of vocational learning (Giddens & Stasz, 1999). Colleges, workplaces and training providers are the loci of vocational learning; schools are not primarily considered thus; it is a mantle that they have had to assume, often to sustain numbers. They are not natural sites for vocational learning; their staff are not, generally speaking, qualified in the vocational area where they are required to teach. The geographer has had to take on the role of a tour operator, the PE teacher the leisure centre manager.

Similarly, prevailing pedagogies differ because, put at its simplest, teaching a student 'how to prepare lamb cutlets' is a very different activity from teaching about the 'causes of the First World War'. The delivery of vocational programmes is predicated upon notions of 'applied learning' and yet there is no real consensus as to what this is (Lucas et al., 2012). Policy documents have placed emphasis on the 'motivational' aspects of 'practical learning' and yet what is required of the learner within truly vocational programmes is 'real' engagement with tasks, work routines and communities of practice. This is nowhere more powerfully illustrated than in the pleas of college lecturers requesting schools not to send them disaffected and disengaged pupils to participate in school/college link programmes, such as the former Increased Flexibilities Programme (Huddleston & Unwin, 2013).

In the past, the terms 'vocational education' and 'vocational qualifications' tended to bind together in an 'unholy alliance' programme that had very different purposes and outcomes. If I want to be a chef, I do not want to have my training labelled as a programme for the disaffected. I want the programme recognised as something of value, which carries occupational currency and which leads ultimately to employment in the sector. Is this any different from a young person who decides to embark upon a programme in veterinary science or architecture? If I have not yet decided upon a possible career route, then the opportunity to sample a range of different options, by way of introduction, should be welcomed. However, the learner should be left in no doubt about the credibility and portability of the qualification. Neither should the learner be compromised in any future choice of career or qualification route.

This argues the case for effective independent advice and guidance around the purposes of qualifications, their content and, most importantly where, or where not, they might lead. Given the pressures on schools and colleges to attract and retain students, and the associated funding implications, this inevitably creates tensions. It is salutary to reflect upon evidence collected over a decade ago across four West Midlands colleges as part of a study on recruitment and retention within GNVQ programmes (Huddleston, 2002, Huddleston & Unwin, 2013) that students applying for popular, and already full, courses were often navigated to alternative options with the suggestion that these were very similar and would lead to the same outcome, when frequently they would not.

Until the full impact of 16–19 Study Programmes is evaluated, possibly not until the reporting of results from 2016 and beyond, it will be impossible to judge how far they have succeeded in offering learners programmes that are well integrated and provide true vocational learning opportunities, rather than being holding bays for those who are neither pursuing academic courses nor work-based apprenticeships. Recent research evidence suggests that there could be rather a lot of them (Maguire, 2015).

Conclusions

A complex reform programme, such as that outlined in the current policy for 16–19 Study Programmes, inevitably brings significant challenges. Such challenges are not new; they have beset full-time 16–19 education policy, arguably from the introduction of ROSLA (Raising of the School Leaving Age) in 1972, but now have been brought into sharper focus since full implementation of RPA in 2015. The retention of young people within education and training post-16 requires a multiplicity of options – not all of these will be vocational – but it should be clearly stated what is and what is not. The minister's original statement (Matthew Hancock, speech to the Sunday Times Festival of Education, Wellington College, June 2014) suggested that "a new, rigorous, ambitious vocational offer from 14 right through to 19 and beyond" would be put in place. Clearly, not everything set out within the Study Programmes meets the criteria suggested by the foregoing discussion for a truly vocational offer.

We have argued that vocational programmes require some important conditions to be in place. The content must be sufficiently work-related to provide the necessary credibility; it should be delivered by those with up-to-date knowledge, skills and experience of the sector. It requires access to real-work contexts and tasks: "vocational learning privileges experiential and active learning with opportunities to engage in authentic tasks and to encounter and learn from experts within communities of practice" (Huddleston, 2011: 43).

So far, it appears that the burden of proof will reside within the design of some new qualifications: Tech levels, Technical certificates and Applied Generals; other aspects of the programmes will be extremely difficult to monitor and quality assure, for example work experience, developing employability skills, 'character', 'attitudes' and 'confidence'. Will simply having something in place be sufficient to justify vocational relevance and meet Ofsted inspection criteria? Since the Association of Colleges (2014) has already indicated that a significant number of work experience placements have to be internal – that is in college environments – it is difficult to see how such a condition could be met. For those learners following programmes below level 2, who are required to spend most of their time on work experience and other work-related activities, vocational relevance and opportunities for progression could be harder to assure.

Names carry powerful connotations; the 'v' word has for too long been associated with the second class rather than with high-quality education and training provision, which in the best cases it assuredly is. This is the result of the misnaming of programmes, courses, routes and pathways as vocational when, according to the criteria suggested earlier, clearly they are not. It does nothing for the credibility of strong vocational qualifications that other non-general qualifications are described and offered by institutions as vocational. Whilst it is recognised that under the conditions set by RPA schools and colleges need to recruit and retain post-16 students, they must be honest in describing accurately what is offered, its purpose and where it might lead. In terms of the title of this chapter 'doing what it says on the tin' may depend upon who is reading the label.

It is too early to say if the proposed Study Programmes will address long-standing problems; more attention appears to have been given to the naming of qualifications and their conditions of approval, but this does not guarantee their successful delivery, in vocational terms, across hundreds of schools and colleges. The 'other' aspects of Study Programmes will be much harder to regulate and quality assure, and there are already capacity issues.

References

Acquah, D. and Huddleston, P. (2014) Challenges and opportunities for vocational education and training in the light of raising the participation age. *Research in Post-Compulsory Education and Training*, 19(1), 1–17.
Association of Colleges (AOC). (2014) *16–19 Study Programmes Survey Report*. London: AOC.
CBI. (2014) *Gateway to Growth – CBI/Pearson Education and Skills Survey 2014*. London: Confederation of British Industry.
DfE. (2012) *Raising the Participation Age (RPA) Regulations: Government Response to Consultation and Plans for Implementation*. London: DfE.
DfE. (2014) *2016 16–19 Performance Tables: Inclusion of Applied General Qualifications*. London: DfE.
DfE. (2015) *16–19 Study Programmes: Departmental Advice for Senior Leadership Teams, Curriculum Planners, Teachers, Trainers and Co-Ordinators on the Planning and Delivery of 16–19 Study Programmes*. London: DfE.
DfES. (2007) *Raising Expectations: Staying in Education and Training Post-16, Cm7065*. London: The Stationery Office.
Ertl, H. and Stasz, C. (2010) Employing and 'employer-led' design? An evaluation of the development of diplomas. *Journal of Education and Work*, 23(4), 301–317.
Felstead, A., Gallie, D. and Green, F. (2002) *Work Skills in Britain, 1986–2001*. London: DfES.
Giddens, B. and Stasz, C. (1999) *Context Matters: Teaching and Learning Skills for Work*. Berkeley: National Center for Research in Vocational Education, University of California.
House of Commons Education and Skills Committee. (2007) *14–19 Diplomas, Fifth Report of the Session 2006–07. HC 249*. London: The Stationery Office.
Huddleston, P. (2002) *'Uncertain Destinies' Student Recruitment and Retention on GNVQ (Intermediate) Programmes*. ESRC SKOPE Research Centre, Universities of Oxford and Warwick, Winter.
Huddleston, P. (2011) *'Vocational Pedagogy: Bringing It All Together?' Open to Ideas: Essays on Education and Skills. National Skills forum/Associate Parliamentary Skills Group*, 42–29. London: Policy Connect.
Huddleston, P. and Fettes, T. (2000) *Vocationalism within General Education: An International Perspective*. Coventry: QCA/CEI.
Huddleston, P. and Laczik, A. (2012) Successes and challenges of employer engagement: The new Diploma qualification. *Journal of Education and Work*, 25(4), 403–421.

Huddleston, P. and Unwin, L. (2013) *Teaching and Learning in Further Education. Diversity and Change*, 4th edition. London: Routledge.

Lave, J. and Wenger, E. (1991) *Situated Learning: Legitimate Peripheral Participation*. New York: Cambridge University Press.

Le Métais, J. (2002) *International Developments in Upper Secondary Education: Context, Provision and Issues*. INCA Thematic Study No. 8, Slough: National Foundation for Educational Research.

Lord, P. (2006) *What Young People Want form the Curriculum (Summary Report)*. Slough: National Foundation for Educational Research.

Lucas, B., Spencer, E. and Claxton, G. (2012) *How to Teach Vocational Education: A Theory of Vocational Pedagogy*. London: City and Guilds Centre for Skills Development.

Maguire, S. (2015) NEET, unemployed, inactive or unknown – why does it matter? *Educational Research*, 57(2), 121–132.

Ofsted. (2014) Transforming 16–19 education and training: The early implementation of 16–19 study programmes. Report Number: 140129.

QCA. (2006) *The Diploma: An Overview of the Qualification*. London: QCA.

Simmons, R. (2008) Raising the age of compulsory education in England: A NEET solution? *British Journal of Educational Studies*, 56(4), 420–439.

Skills Commission. (2015) *Guide to the Skills System*. London: Skills Commission.

Skills Commission. (undated) *Teacher Training in Vocational Education*. London: Skills Commission.

Stanton, G. (2004) The organisation of full-time 14–19 provision in the state sector. Nuffield Review of 14–19 Education and Training Working Paper 13.

Stanton, G. (2006) Rhetoric and reality: Vocational options and current educational policy. Centre for Guidance Studies, Occasional Paper.

Stanton, G. and Bailey, B. (2005) In search of VET. Research Paper 62, December, ESRC SKOPE

Stasz, C. and Wright, S. (2004) Outcomes and processes in vocational learning. A review of the literature. Modelling a vocational learning system for the 21st century. Learning and Skills Research Centre Report. London: LSRC.

Tuomi-Grohn, T. and Engerstrom, Y. (eds.) (2003) *Between School and Work. New Perspectives on Boundary Crossing*. Oxford: Pergamon.

UKCES. (2014) *UK Commission's Employer Skills Survey 2013: UK Results*. London: UK Commission for Employment and Skills.

Wolf, A. (2011) *Review of Vocational Education – The Wolf Report*. London: Department for Education.

Young, M. (2003) National qualifications as a global phenomenon: A comparative perspective. *Journal of Education and Work*, 16(3), 223–37. http://www.aqa.org.uk/subjects/business-subjects/tech-level/business-marketing/statement-of-purpose

6 Links between concepts of skill, concepts of occupation and the training system
A case study of Australia

Erica Smith

Introduction

This paper explores the nexus between the concepts of vocation and of occupational identity and their links to the training system. Vocational education and training (VET), and apprenticeship systems in particular, have grown from concepts of occupation. It is self-evident that VET prepares, or upskills, people for work, and therefore the training must relate to job roles, whether broadly or narrowly defined. However, the processes by which students receive training that is high quality, rigorous and government-funded are not clearly defined. One yardstick that can be applied is that training is much more likely to be privileged (in terms of training provision, rigorous curriculum and government funding) when a job is considered to be an 'occupation'. The development of occupational identity is taken for granted, for example in traditional 'trade' apprenticeships in Australia or the UK trainers and teachers, employers, trade unions and policy makers share a commitment to the apprenticed trades as distinct and valuable occupations.

What are the implications of these issues for the training system as a whole? In Australia, as in the UK, the availability of qualifications has kept pace with the structural changes in the economy as a whole (i.e. with the relative shift to service industries), yet some occupations and some qualifications are less respected than others. This paper uses recent research carried out in Australia to show the potential effects on workers and their access to training of conceptions of 'worth' in work.

Background

Apprenticeships and traineeships

The Australian apprenticeship system grew from European traditions and was formally established with sets of qualifications in the immediate post-Second World War period. The sense of 'being' a carpenter, a mechanic or a hairdresser is part and parcel of the process of thinking about a career in a craft or trade, applying for an apprenticeship, undergoing the training period and the eventual practice as a 'skilled' worker (Brown, 1997).

In the Australian VET system, apprenticeships and traineeships are very important. They account for a little under one-fifth of the 1.79 million annual enrolments in VET qualifications (National Centre for Vocational Education Research, 2015). This proportion has been declining for several years, as will be seen later in the paper. Apprentices and trainees in Australia, unlike the situation in some other countries (Smith & Brennan Kemmis, 2013) are always employed; part-time workers and adults are eligible, as well as young people in full-time work. Apprentices and trainees undertake formal training which may be by attendance at a TAFE Institute (the public provider) or a private registered training organisation (RTO) or may consist of formalised training in the workplace, which is monitored and assessed by TAFE or another RTO. The government funds the formal training and also provides employment incentives to employers. About 15 per cent of apprentices and trainees are employed through Group Training Organisations which, through employing apprentices and trainees and then 'leasing' to employers, perform a type of 'labour hire' function, relieving employers of administrative burdens while providing added pastoral care elements (Bush & Smith, 2007).

Traineeships were established in Australia in the second half of the 1980s as a result of a deliberate government policy to expand access to contracted training opportunities (i.e. apprentice-like arrangements) to a broader set of industry areas and to women (Kirby, 1985). The majority of traineeships are in areas where apprenticeships did not previously exist (e.g. retail, IT, business and aged care) and generally last for 12–18 months rather than the three to four years of an apprenticeship. While trainees are still more numerous than apprentices (National Centre for Vocational Education Research, 2014), their numbers have recently fallen, as will be explained in the following sections.

There is a comparative dearth of scholarly work about traineeships. Early work focused primarily on perceived poor quality and employer abuse of the system in order to access funding advantages (e.g. Schofield, 2000). Later work focuses on the use which employers make of traineeship qualifications to lift their companies' quality standards (e.g. Booth *et al.*, 2005). Towards the end of the first decade of the twenty-first century, broader studies began to be carried out which looked more generally at the quality of traineeships (Bowman *et al.*, 2005; Smith et al., 2009).

Occupations and qualifications

In the Australian VET system before the mid-1980s, most VET was provided for jobs which had an apprenticeship attached to them, with a minor but still substantial stream of qualifications which people undertook full time before commencing full-time employment (e.g. 'secretarial studies') or upskilled at 'night school' while working (e.g. building industry 'clerk of works'). Qualifications for other work began to be introduced in the 1980s – for example in retail and other service-sector industries, or in non-apprenticed jobs in fields (such as manufacturing) which also had apprenticeships – but this process, known as 'training reform', met with opposition from those who believed these changes somehow denied or interfered with the integrity of occupations (e.g. Buchanan, 2006). Such resistance was stiffened by the establishment of 'traineeships', which attracted types of government support and training funding previously reserved for apprenticeships. It was not helped that this new pool of government funding attracted some less-than-ethical training providers, as mentioned earlier.

Many occupations regarded as 'low skilled' have only recently been assigned qualifications in Australia, as the qualifications were often developed to accompany traineeships rather than being pre-existing. Compared with long-standing curricula established for traditional trades, occupations such as retail, housekeeping, cleaning and security have only recently accrued formal qualifications. VET qualifications are now gathered together into around 80 occupation- or industry-focused, competency-based 'Training Packages'; the roll-out of these 'Training Packages' began in 1997. The curriculum in such Training Package qualifications is often perceived as being relatively 'thin' (Smith, 2002), with the 'underpinning knowledge' section of the units of competency being slight compared with traditional trades which have a long-standing existing body of knowledge. Many newer qualifications are often delivered primarily on-the-job; if delivered poorly, underpinning knowledge may be confined to that needed for that particular situational circumstance and theoretical constructs may not be covered (Smith & Smith, 2009). However, more recently, Training Packages have included a greater emphasis on knowledge components.

Occupational identity

Valenduc *et al.* (2007) noted that occupational identity has become increasingly common as a topic for study. Brown (2004, 1997), referring to Dewey's work, describes occupational identity as "a 'home' with psychological, social and ideological 'anchors'". He states that while occupational identities may be fixed through history in some cases, individuals also have the opportunity to shape occupational identity either for themselves or for a group of workers. In his study of engineering workers, Brown (2004) noted that while some were firmly attached to the occupation, others were just 'passing through', while still others found their identity primarily through their employing company.

Traineeship occupations in Australia are currently of lower status than apprenticed occupations. The presence of a long-established apprenticeship qualification in itself may create a collective sense of occupational identity which adds to the individual sense of occupational identity. Smith (2000), in her study of apprentices, trainees and other young workers, noted that the apprentices identified strongly with their occupation, while the trainees tended to identify with their employing organisation and industry rather than their particular job role. The lesser sense of occupational identity, along with the lack of institutional support, for example by trade unions, has left the traineeship system vulnerable to attack, as Smith (2009) predicted.

Smith (2009) began to explore this topic using Brown's framework (Brown, 2004), through examination of occupational identity at the level of the individual, organization and society. She used data from a research project on quality in traineeships, through the lens of detailed research in two traineeship qualifications: one in cleaning and one in general construction (non-apprenticed). She found that, at an individual level, some workers may identify more closely with the organisation than the occupation; they may not value their traineeship qualification very highly. She also found that some trainees were not aware that they were enrolled in traineeships. At the organisational level, she found that some employers were inexperienced in traineeship management and that this was a barrier to the development of an occupational identity. In the construction area, she found that trade unions had actively opposed traineeships. At the level of society as a whole, she found that the jobs covered by traineeships were of lower status than related jobs covered by apprenticeships.

Recently in the UK, Fuller and Unwin (2013) have used the concept of occupational identity to critique the current apprenticeship system. The UK system was expanded in a similar way to the Australian system to include jobs not covered by the 'traditional' trade apprenticeship system. Fuller and Unwin argue that apprenticeship should by its nature include access to membership of an occupation, and that the UK system, which they see as having qualifications at differing levels and which are, in their view, not well-matched to readily identifiable occupational roles as traditional apprenticeships are (e.g. fitter, carpenter), is therefore inappropriate. They do acknowledge, however, that the 'traditional' apprenticeship system in some countries including the UK is 'highly gendered' and therefore is not unproblematic (Fuller & Unwin, 2013: 7).

New research relating to this topic

The paper goes on to draw on data from recent pieces of research which shed light on this topic. The first is a project analysing the effects of changes in funding in the State of Victoria on training for certain occupations (Project 1: Guthrie *et al.*, 2014). The second is a three-year project looking at the concept of skill in work (Project 2: Smith *et al.*, 2015). The section concludes with an analysis of the decline in traineeships as a result of the de-funding of training for certain occupations by commonwealth (federal) and state governments alike, as well as the effects of this on training for certain occupations.

Project 1: Funding for training in Victoria

Project 1, funded by Service Skills Victoria, showed that the topic of occupational identity and its association with training became concretised in quite a stark manner through Australian federal and state policies in relation to the funding of training. While the word 'occupation' is not explicitly used in policy documents, the words 'valued career', 'valued job' or jobs with 'public value' are frequently used. These terms began to be used in a government 'expert panel' report on apprenticeships in 2011 (Department of Employment, Education and Workplace Relations [DEEWR], 2011). The panel was dominated by representatives from, or associated with, traditional trade unions and deliberately advocated the de-funding of traineeships. The panel advocated that only 'eligible' apprentices and trainees could be funded: those on a specialised occupations list drawn up by Skills Australia,[1] those which represented a 'valued career' and those that could 'be traded in the marketplace'. In fact the occupations on this list were all 'traditional' apprenticeship occupations, apart from aged care. The eligibility list was to be 'guarded' by a 'national custodian'. The government did not agree to the national custodian idea and did not explicitly agree to de-funding traineeships. However, the de-funding happened in successive federal budgets and mid-year financial statements during 2012–14, as employment incentives were reduced for various categories of traineeships, but not for 'traditional' apprenticeships. It is interesting to note that for the majority of this time, a Labour (social democratic) rather than Liberal (conservative) government was in office at the national level.

The project, which combined analysis of national and state-level VET data with interviews and focus groups with employers and training providers in the service industries in Victoria, found that funding changes in Victoria worked together with the federal changes in funding described earlier to make the delivery of qualifications virtually impossible in some occupational areas. It described how the government of the State of Victoria used a state budget to announce its own contribution to the de-dismantling of training for non-apprenticed occupations. A conservative government in power from 2011–2014 needed to reduce a 'blow-out' in spending due to the previous government's expansion of the training market which opened up all government funding to private training providers. The quality of many providers was very low, which lead to the reputation of the whole VET system suffering (Department of Education & Training, 2015). There were two main ways in which funding was reduced: first by drastically reducing hourly rates of funding per student for some qualifications and second by removing the special government payments to TAFE, the public provider.

In announcing the new schedule of funding rates for qualifications, the Victorian government used these words: "Subsidy rates[2] for VET courses will be refocused to better target areas of greatest public benefit and future jobs growth" (Government of Victoria, 2012). Full funding was retained and, in some cases, increased for qualifications relating to apprenticed occupations, but was reduced for other occupations, in some cases to $1.50 per hour per student, compared to $12.50 for some apprenticeship qualifications. At $1.50, it was not possible to offer training except by requiring a large contribution from the student, and many training providers stopped offering courses in areas such as retail, front-of-house hospitality, fitness and business services. This meant that traineeships were no longer offered in these occupations. An advent of a Labour government in late 2014 has led to the restoration of some funding for TAFE Institutes, but no action has yet been taken about the inequitable distribution of funding across qualifications. The research found that in the State of Victoria, training funding for jobs such as retail assistant has virtually disappeared, particularly in some rural and remote locations. A similar, albeit less radical, pattern has been followed in other states and territories.

The funding changes have adversely affected jobs more often undertaken by women compared with those more often undertaken by men. As has been mentioned earlier in this paper, the Kirby report of 1985 set out partly to redress the gender imbalance with regard to availability of training, but in Victoria, the Kirby gains were rapidly reversed. Table 6.1, adapted from a table from the project report, shows clearly how, in nearly every case, the rates for funding in place after

Table 6.1 State of Victoria. Funded enrolments and funding rates 2011 and 2013, selected courses ordered by proportion of female enrolments

Qualification	Total enrolments 2011	% Female enrolments 2011	Total enrolments 2013	% Female enrolments 2013	2011 funding per student hour	2013 funding per student hour
Certificate III in Bricklaying/Blocklaying (apprenticeship)	1,174	0.2	1,647	0.4	$11.35	$11.50
Certificate III in Plumbing (apprenticeship)	3,661	0.5	5,176	0.5	$12.30	$12.50
Certificate III in Carpentry (apprenticeship)	7,621	1.8	9,034	1.0	$11.35	$11.50
Certificate III in Telecommunications	256	3.9	298	3.4	$8.09	$9.00
Certificate III in Competitive Manufacturing	1,133	21	1,749	24	$8.99	$10.00*
Certificate II in Agriculture	1,620	24	1,380	32	$11.18	$8.00
Diploma of Hospitality	3,688	43	1,044	51	$7.04	$2.00
Certificate II in Hospitality	12,324	62	3,922	66	$9.32	$1.50
Certificate III in Hospitality	13,999	63	5,903	62	$8.99	$1.50
Certificate II in Retail	11,983	64	1,709	63	$7.46	$1.50
Certificate III in Retail	12,820	68	5,329	66	$7.19	$1.50
Certificate III in Events	1,083	74	205	82	$8.99	$1.50
Certificate III in Hairdressing (apprenticeship)	3,610	94	4,815	94	$9.46	$10.50
Certificate III in Beauty Services	1,308	99	2,108	95	$8.99	$7.00

the cuts had a close positive correlation to the proportion of men enrolled in the qualifications. The exceptions are the apprenticed trade of hairdresser and the related area of beauty services. The two shaded columns indicate the proportion of female enrolments in 2011 and then in 2103 after the major impact of the cuts was felt. The table also indicates the huge drop in people in training in the occupations most affected by the funding cuts. It should also be mentioned at this point that retail and hospitality combined, which suffered most under these cuts, were the largest employing sectors in the State of Victoria at this time.

Project 2: Undervalued skill in occupations

The second project, funded by the Australian Research Council, looked at nine occupations which are seen in Australia as 'unskilled' or 'low-skilled'. The occupations which were seen as unskilled or low-skilled were hotel reception worker (guest service agent), cleaner, security operator, concrete products operator, sewing machinist, waiter, chef and retail (non-supermarket) assistant. Two of the occupations studied, metal fitter and machinist and chef, are traditionally seen as skilled in Australia, i.e. they are apprenticed trades.

The project involved a number of phases, including interviews with senior stakeholders in the Australian industrial relations and vocational education and training systems; occupational studies, including interviews with stakeholders in the occupation; two company case studies for each occupation; and a detailed and structured examination of the relevant qualification compared with the skills uncovered in the occupation during the project. In the first phase (national stakeholders), interviewees displayed a nuanced understanding of skill (Smith *et al.*, 2014). While recognising the role that qualifications played, they did not see qualifications as defining skill or as the markers of the presence or absence of skill. The major conclusion to be drawn from the analysis was that, overwhelmingly, respondents saw skill in all jobs, albeit to varying extents. There was also a sense that they did not like to see jobs 'looked down upon'. They were conscious, however, to varying extents of the official positions they were supposed to espouse. Government VET officials in two states explicitly said that in making decisions that were based on whether jobs were more or less skilled (for funding purposes), they needed to adhere to their departments' official views, which derived in both cases from national classifications prepared by the Australian Bureau of Statistics, but they explained that they held quite different views themselves.

The occupational case studies showed that the so-called unskilled occupations that were examined contained a great deal of both technical and non-technical skill; the jobs were often hidden from public view, or conversely were in such plain sight that their everydayness belied their skill content. With one exception, they did not require qualifications in order to practice. When the qualifications were systematically examined, we found that all were missing important elements of skill that had been uncovered in our research. The jobs often had very good career prospects, but the career paths were not well known outside the industry and sometimes not well known inside the organisations. The occupations often had workforces that were marginalised in some way: either undereducated, migrant or student workers undertook the jobs. These factors ('hidden skills, hidden career paths, hidden qualifications and hidden workforces') combined to make the jobs appear unattractive and low in status. Significantly, most of the jobs were funded at very low levels following the Victorian training funding cuts.

A comparison of these seven occupations with the two so-called skilled jobs examined in the project was instructive. People in the 'skilled jobs' were much better able to explain and articulate the skills involved in their work: this was the result of the curricula for those jobs being much better developed and therefore providing 'names' for the activities in the occupations. These people regarded themselves as skilled (yet, interestingly, did not denigrate those who worked alongside them in different jobs as being unskilled). While it might be expected that people regarded themselves as being in the occupations for a long time, if not for life, in fact we found that companies often looked to people in those occupations as potential senior management material, i.e. it was expected that they would move out of the occupation. Interestingly, though, and particularly with regard to the job of fitter and machinist, managers reported that trade unions' positions on job demarcation often prevented the fitters from advancing readily to middle management positions. With relation to the qualifications, the latter tended to reflect the work undertaken in the occupations better than did the other seven so-called 'unskilled' occupations, although there were other flaws in the qualifications. It was concluded that the relatively inadequate curriculum, which in the case of the seven 'unskilled' or 'low skilled' occupations was developed through the post-1997 medium of Training Packages, has probably contributed to these occupations being 'looked down on' (Smith *et al.*, 2015).

The Australia-wide decline in numbers of people in traineeship occupations

We now move to an examination of the current statistics on apprenticeships and traineeships. There has been a rapid decline in traineeship numbers since the publishing of the expert panel report (DEEWR, 2011). Apart from the cuts in state government funding mentioned earlier through the example of the State of Victoria, the commonwealth government, as previously mentioned, has reduced the financial incentives which were previously offered to employers who employ trainees and apprentices upon completion of the contracts of training. While apprenticeship employment incentives have not been reduced at all, funding for traineeships has been reduced, again through budget cuts rather than debate. This reduction has happened incrementally, through progressive reductions in successive budgets: commencement and progression incentives were removed, leaving only completion incentives; incentives for existing workers moving onto traineeships were removed, leaving incentives only for newly employed workers; and incentives for apprentices and trainees employed by group training organisations were removed. Many large employers who have trainees now do not even claim the small amount of employment incentive that remains (e.g. Smith *et al.*, 2015).

Figures produced by the national VET data and research agency, the National Centre for Vocational Education Research (NCVER, 2014), show that the number of apprentices and trainees decreased by 10.3 per cent in 2013 alone, from 346,600 to 311,000 students. Commencements decreased by 25.9 per cent; trade commencements (i.e. apprenticeships) decreased by only 2.3 per cent, while non-trade commencements (i.e. traineeships) decreased by 37.5 per cent. As a proportion of all VET students, apprentices and trainees comprised 17.4 per cent of the government-funded VET student population in 2014, down from 18.7 per cent in 2013 (NCVER, 2015).

It was only a few years ago that Australia had over 400,000 apprentices and trainees and was able to compare its ratio of apprentices/trainees to the workforce as a whole with that of Germany (Walters, 2003). Interviews with employers and training providers in Project 1 showed that it was a combination of the removal of federal government incentives together with the reduction in state funding for the actual training delivery that led to this rapid decline in numbers. The latter reduction meant not only that training became prohibitively expensive but also that many training providers actually ceased offering training in some occupational areas because they would have lost so much money doing it. Some training providers closed down. Certain geographical areas were adversely affected by this, leaving no available training for employers or individual learners to access.

Analysis and discussion

Vallas (1990) has warned that there are far-reaching implications of hasty and possibly inaccurate judgments about some jobs being skilled and others being categorised as unskilled, and these implications have been fully realised in the Australian context, with some occupations being marginalised. The public discourse has revolved around the value of the actual job rather than the amount of skill supposedly present in the job.

It need hardly be mentioned that the social construction of skill is a strong factor at play in this domain. It has long been argued that 'skill' is often socially constructed and the same applies to the construction of 'occupations'. Similarly, it is self-evident that the jobs that tend to be done by women (at least those serviced by the VET sector) are less often known as 'occupations' than those that are more likely to be done by men. The matter of gender and VET is widely discussed (e.g. Fuller & Unwin, 2013; Niemeyer & Colley, 2015). However, the fact that 'women's work' is less valued than 'men's work' is often problematised only to the extent of an argument that women's choices are normatively constrained and an advocacy that more women should go into jobs that are more often done by men (e.g. Simon & Clarke, 2015), rather than thinking about why it is that men's jobs are considered to be more skilled than women's.

A few years ago, the UN Economic and Social Council Commission on the Status of Women made this point in its agreed recommendations (55th session, February-March 2011). It recommended that "public resources in education, training, science, technology and research (should) equally benefit women and men, girls and boys", and that countries should "work to eliminate occupational and sectoral segregation and the gender pay gap by recognising the value of sectors that have large numbers of women workers, such as care and other service workers". In a recent Australian paper, Thompson (2015), however, argues that while some service occupations are worthwhile (she cites those in health and community services) others should not have their training funded because they offer 'shallow career ladders' and there is reportedly no return on investment for qualifications gained.

It is regrettable that training opportunities for many occupations in Australia have been reduced. What is perhaps more important is that traineeships and apprenticeships represent jobs as well as training. This was well recognised by the Kirby Report which was in fact the output of a 'Committee of Inquiry into labour market programs'. Similarly, traditional apprenticeships have always been viewed as job creation programmes as much as training programs. While not all trainees and not all apprentices are young people, traineeships and apprenticeships have always been important routes into the full-time labour market for young people. It can hardly be a coincidence that the trend in youth unemployment (15–24) in Australia has moved upwards since the beginning of 2012 – moving from around 11 per cent at that time to around 14 per cent in 2015. It is recognised, however, that many caveats need to be made when discussing employment and unemployment figures for young people due to their particularly complex engagement with education and the labour market.

The issues raised in this paper have yet to be fully discussed both in policy circles and in the academy. The optimistic developments of the 1980s with relation to equal access to training for groups in society and for all occupations have been so rapidly reversed in Australia that it has possibly prevented the full extent of the crisis being recognised. It is clear that interest groups have campaigned for the changes to happen, as was evident in the membership and the consultations associated with the expert panel report on apprenticeship (DEEWR, 2011) which began the process of, or at least gave a justification for, the funding reductions. It is comparatively easy to see why trade unions representing workers in occupations recognised widely as 'skilled' fought for their status, and for training funding to be retained at the expense of other occupations. The occupations that have been most affected are those which are weakly organised into unions. It is possible to understand why some in society might wish to return to an era when craft work was valorised. But it is difficult to understand why governments have so readily implemented developments that have removed training funding from so many jobs that are so important in the twenty-first century economy. The research in Project 2 showed that senior stakeholders in government and other organisations had quite a sophisticated understanding of skill in work and therefore of value in occupations. And yet their governments had, by the end of our project, set back the cause of occupational equality considerably. A depressing reality may simply be that the arguments mounted in government documents for not funding, or for under-funding, certain qualifications were simply offered as justification for withdrawing funding from training for some occupations. These occupations were weakly organised and also happen to be those least valued in Australian society; hence a judgment may have been made that public opinion would not rally behind those occupations. The fact that they are also among the most common occupations in modern Australia meant that a greater amount of expenditure could be saved.

Acknowledgements

The author would like to thank co-researchers in the projects used as the basis for this chapter Andy Smith, Ian Hampson, Anne Junor, Hugh Guthrie, Pam Every and Sally Burt.

Notes

1 This list had originally been drawn up for migration purposes but then began to be used for other contexts in VET policy.
2 Perhaps significantly, this was the first time that a government had used the word 'subsidy' instead of 'funding' to describe government funding for training. The term has rapidly been adopted throughout the system.

References

Booth, R., Roy, S., Jenkins, H., Clayton, B. and Sutcliffe, S. (2005) *Workplace Training Practices in the Residential Aged Care Sector*. Adelaide: National Centre for Vocational Education Research (NCVER).
Bowman, K., Stanwick, S. and Blythe, A. (2005) *Factors Pertaining to Quality Outcomes of Shorter Duration Apprenticeships and Traineeships*. Adelaide: NCVER.
Brown, A. (1997) A dynamic model in occupational identity formation, in A. Brown (ed.) *Promoting Vocational Education and Training: European Perspectives*. Tampere: EUROPROF. http://www.leeds.ac.uk/educol/documents/000000312.htm (Accessed 26 May 2016)
Brown, A. (2004) Engineering identities. *Career Development International*, 9(3), 254–273.
Buchanan, J. (2006) *From Skill Shortages to Decent Work: The Role of Better Skill Ecosystems*. Sydney: NSW Department of Education and Training.
Bush, A. and Smith, E. (2007) Group training organisations: Bellwethers or shepherds? Evolution, revolution or status quo? The new context for VET, 10th Conference of the Australian VET Research Association Group, 11–13 April, Victoria University, Footscray Park.
Department of Education and Training – Victoria (DET). (2015) *Review of Quality Assurance in Victoria's VET System*. Melbourne: DET.
Department of Employment, Education and Workplace Relations (DEEWR). (2011) *A Shared Responsibility: Apprenticeships for the 21st Century*. Canberra: DEEWR.
Fuller, A. and Unwin, L. (2013) *Apprenticeship and the Concept of Occupation*. London: The Gatsby Charitable Foundation.
Government of Victoria. (2012) *Refocusing Vocational Training in Victoria*. Melbourne: Department of Education and Early Childhood Development.

Guthrie, H., Smith, E., Burt, S. and Every, P. (2014) *Review of the Effects of Funding Approaches on Service Skills Qualifications and Delivery in Victoria*. Melbourne: Service Skills Victoria.

Kirby, P. (1985) *Report of the Committee of Inquiry into Labour Market Programs*. Canberra: Australian Government Publishing Service.

National Centre for Vocational Education Research (NCVER). (2014) *Australian Vocational Education and Training (VET) Statistics: Apprentices and Trainees 2013*. Adelaide: NCVER.

National Centre for Vocational Education Research. (2015) *Australian Vocational Education and Training (VET) Statistics: Government Funded Students and Courses 2014*. Adelaide: NCVER.

Niemeyer, B. and Colley, H. (2015) Why do we need (another) special issue on gender and VET? Editorial. *Journal of Vocational Education and Training*, 17(1), 1–10.

Schofield, K. (2000) *Delivering Quality: Report of the Independent Review of the Quality of Training in Victoria's Apprenticeship & Traineeship System*. Melbourne: Office of Post Compulsory Education & Training.

Simon, L. and Clarke, K. (2015) Apprenticeships should work for women too: Supporting meaningful exploration of 'non-traditional careers' for young women. Architectures for apprenticeship: Achieving economic and social goals, 6th INAP (Network on Innovative Apprenticeship) Conference, Federation University Australia, Ballarat, 1–2 September.

Smith, E. (2000) Young people's learning about work in their first year of full-time work. Doctoral thesis, University of Technology, Sydney.

Smith, E. (2002) Training packages: Debates around a new curriculum system. *Issues in Educational Research*, 12(1), 64–84.

Smith, E. (2009) Occupational identity in Australian traineeships: An initial exploration. Apprenticeship: A Successful Tradition and Innovation of School-to-Work Transitions: INAP (Network on Innovative Apprenticeship) Conference, 17–18 September, Turin.

Smith, E. and Brennan Kemmis, R. (2013) *Towards a Model Apprenticeship Framework: A Comparative Analysis of National Apprenticeship Systems*. New Delhi: ILO. http://www.ilo.org/newdelhi/whatwedo/publications/WCMS_234728/lang—en/index.htm

Smith, E., Comyn, P., Brennan Kemmis, R. and Smith, A. (2009) *High Quality Traineeships: Identifying what Works*. Adelaide: NCVER.

Smith, E. and Smith, A. (2009) Making training core business: Enterprise registered training organisations in Australia. *Journal of Vocational Education and Training*, 61(3), 287–306.

Smith, E., Smith, A., Hampson, I. and Junor, A. (2014) What do senior figures in Australian VET and industrial relations think about the concept of skill in work? Informing Changes in VET Policy and Practice: The Central Role of Research, 17th annual AVETRA Conference, 22–24 April, Surfers Paradise, Queensland.

Smith, E., Smith, A., Junor, A. and Hampson, I. (2015) *Recognising the Skill in Jobs Traditionally Considered Unskilled*. Sydney: Manufacturing Skills Australia. http://www.mskills.org.au/industry-intelligence/info/research-publications

Smith, E., Smith, A., Walker, A. and Costa, B. (2015) How do qualifications delivered by enterprises contribute to improved skill levels and other benefits for companies, workers and the nation? Project summary for consultation.

Thompson, S. (2015) Women, work and poor pay. *Australian TAFE Teacher*, 49(3), 24–26.
Valenduc, G., Vendramin, P., Krings, B-J. and Nierling, L. (2007) Occupational case studies: Synthesis report & comparative analysis. *WORKS Project*. http://www.ftu-namur.org/fichiers/WORKS-D11-final.pdf
Vallas, S.P. (1990) The concept of skill: A critical review. *Work and Occupations*, 17(4), 449–482.
Walters, C. (2003) Keynote address, Changing Face of VET: Sixth Annual Conference of the Australian VET Research Association. Sydney, 9–11 April.

7 Training of FE teachers with occupational/vocational experiences
An approach using collaboration and evidence-based research

Sai Loo

Introduction

The intention of this chapter[1] is to provide an approach to the training of teachers (especially those who have vocational or occupational experiences) in the further education (FE) sector. This sector has the following teaching settings: FE colleges, voluntary and community-sector organizations, commercial organizations and independent training providers, adult and community learning providers, industry, specialist colleges, armed and uniformed services, prisons and offending learning organizations and other public-sector organizations (Education & Training Foundation, 2014). In 2013–14, nearly 68 per cent of the provisions in this diverse sector were occupation-related (Frontier Economics Limited, 2014, Table 15).

Furthermore, two other aspects have highlighted the relevance to rethink teacher education in the sector. The first relates to the recent emphasis on vocational training from *The Wolf Report* (Department for Education, 2011), the *Richard Review of Apprenticeships* (Department for Business, Innovation and Skills [BIS], 2012a), the *Lingfield Report* (BIS, 2012b) to the Commission on Adult Vocational Teaching and Learning (Learning and Skills Improvement Service [LSIS], 2013a) and culminating in the establishment of the Centre for Vocational Education Research in March 2015. The second aspect refers to the international spotlight on the complexities of teaching (Tatto, 2013).

These two aspects on teaching and vocationalism must be viewed in the contexts of FE in England. Despite the importance policy makers place on teaching (DfE, 2010), in England, FE teachers are not mandated to acquire a teaching qualification (BIS, 2012b), though teachers are required to undertake 30 hours of continuous professional development per year (BIS, 2012b). The occupational experiences of FE teachers distinguish them from teachers in the compulsory education sectors. Therefore the occupational/disciplinary experiences and knowledge of these teachers along with their pedagogic activities should be included in their teacher education. Bearing in mind the earlier contexts, this chapter argues for a collaborative (i.e. reflective peer review) and evidence-based (i.e. inclusion of disciplinary and pedagogic experiences through research) approach to teacher education, where at present, such practices are inconsistent and under-developed.

The second section relates to relevant theoretical frameworks and the third section highlights related empirical studies. The fourth section discusses the findings in relation to the foci of the chapter and the final section offers insights and implications.

'Knowledge' theoretical frameworks

This section is delineated using two groups of literature sources: the 'curriculum-related' and the 'typologists'. In the first 'curriculum-related' group, 'powerful knowledge' is offered by Young (2013) as a way of focusing on the significance of knowledge in a curriculum such as teacher education in the FE sector where this chapter argues for the inclusion of occupational/disciplinary knowledge alongside pedagogic knowledge. Young uses Bernstein's (1990) binary classification of vertical (theoretical) and horizontal (tacit and everyday) knowledge. Bernstein uses recontextualisation as a process to explain how vertical knowledge is transmitted via "selection, sequence, pace, and relations with other subjects" (Bernstein, 1990: 185) in a pedagogic setting. Barnett (2006) uses recontextualisation processes – reclassificatory and pedagogic – to delineate vocational teaching and learning and Evans *et al.* (2010) draw from the previous sources to offer four recontextualisation processes and to explain how knowledge is acquired and applied. These processes are 'content' (where theoretical knowledge is selected for learners' learning), 'pedagogic' (where theoretical and everyday knowledge is included in the curriculum), 'workplace' (where learners learn whilst working) and 'learner' (where they use strategies to integrate to use and apply theoretical and work-related knowledge).

The two generic forms of knowledge provide a way of thinking about how the complex varieties of pedagogic practices relating to FE teachers may be included in teacher training and the different types of recontextualisation offer ways of understanding how FE teachers with occupational experiences negotiate teaching and learning processes. The next part of this section provides a more nuanced understanding of teacher knowledge.

In the second group, the 'typologists' offer a wider variation of 'teaching' knowledge. Shulman (1987: 8–9) provides a classification of seven types of pedagogic knowledge ranging from content knowledge (knowledge and skills for learning), curriculum knowledge ('tools of the trade', e.g. knowledge of teaching resources), general pedagogical knowledge (strategies surrounding classroom management), pedagogical content knowledge (how content and teaching are organized, represented and used for specific learners), knowledge of learners (needs and characteristics), knowledge of educational contexts and knowledge of educational values. Even though this classification centres on compulsory learners in the US, it does offer a way of engaging with teaching knowledge in FE in other countries, especially where teaching training is usually focused on the generic aspects of teaching knowledge such as general pedagogical knowledge and curriculum knowledge, due partly to the diversity of the curricula and the lack of expertise by teacher educators to cover all the disciplines. Verloop *et al.'s* (2001) typology does cross over with Shulman's in areas such as subject matter, students and their learning, curriculum and instructional techniques and areas relating to compulsory education. However, Verloop *et al.'s* approach is more focused on teachers' interactive cognitions and with a greater emphasis on learners. This typology is especially relevant due to the diversity of FE pedagogic activities and learners, though both typologies have not given sufficient emphasis to the tacit elements of teaching. Loughran *et al.* (2003: 856) attempt to codify teachers' professional knowledge using their 12 'Principles of teaching for quality learning' where they "identify and articulate important and hitherto hidden aspects of their practice". Some of these practices such as sharing intellectual control with learners and encouraging learners to learn from peers are relevant to FE as the learners cover a wide range in terms of ages, experiences and needs. Nevertheless, insufficient emphasis has been placed on teachers' biographical experiences especially occupational practices, which are distinctive to FE teachers. Clandinin (1985) offers a space for the inclusion of FE teachers' occupational know-how with her concept of 'personal practical knowledge'. In this conception, teachers' personal and professional (for the purposes of this chapter, teaching and occupational) experiences, including emotional and moralistic elements, are defined. The expansion of Clandinin's 'personal practical knowledge' for the purposes of this chapter at least opens up spaces for discussion of teachers' occupational experiences in teacher education.

Methods

The empirical findings on which this chapter is based result from two projects which were funded by the Work-Based Learning for Education Professionals Centre, UCL Institute of Education, University College London. The Higher Education Academy funded the centre. The projects were approved by the institution, and they adhered to the British Educational Research Association ethical guidelines. The first project studied the types and application of teacher knowledge in the FE sector (Loo, 2012), while the second investigated a structured collaborative approach to supporting FE teachers' pedagogic activities via digitally recorded teaching sessions (Loo, 2013).

The first project employed a questionnaire survey and semi-structured, one-to-one interviews (of varying lengths of 45–90 minutes), and the second project used digital recordings of volunteer teachers from FE in their teaching activities involving similar learners over three different sessions. This approach was employed in order to prevent abnormal learner behaviour resulting from the use of digital recording equipment. A questionnaire survey was also administered in the second project. Once the recordings were captured, each teacher chose a recording which best illustrated the teaching contexts and submitted this to a peer-review process in focus groups. These groups discussed the teaching activities using a multimodality framework (Kress, 2010) and reflective peer-review (Pollard *et al.*, 2008) approach. All the volunteers were former trainee teachers on the Postgraduate Certificate of Education (Post-compulsory/FE) (PGCE) course at the same institution from different cohorts. The principal investigator of the projects was a tutor of the PGCE programme. In the first project, there were eight volunteers and six volunteers in the second one with five participants taking part in both projects. The combined total number was nine.

Of the nine participants, five were females and four males with two in the 30s age group, two in the 40s and five in the 50s. Of the teaching settings, four were in FE colleges, four in adult and community and one in HE. They had differing lengths of teaching experiences ranging from 3 to 28 years. Of the nine volunteers, five were teaching full-time and four were working part-time. Their different disciplines included art, biology, dance, dental hygiene, health and social care, information technology, journalism, life skills, mathematics, palmistry, physics, psychology and radio production, though the participants were not necessarily limited to one discipline. More significantly, participants' life and occupational experiences included being a civil servant, health and social worker, architect, printmaker, dental hygienist, community worker, graphic designer, homeopath, palmist and reflexologist along with having lived abroad in places such as Japan, Malta, South Africa, Australia, Switzerland and the US.

The findings of the two projects were analysed using qualitative analytical approaches that included noting patterns, themes and trends, clustering of items into categories, using narratives for rich descriptions and interpreting the data (Cohen *et al.*, 2000). Salient details of the participants from the questionnaire and interviews are featured in Table 7.1. These findings are used in this chapter to provide a new direction to FE teacher training where it is inconsistent and under-developed as regards integrating disciplinary and pedagogic knowledge.

Table 7.1 Details of participants

Participant Gender Age Project participation	Teaching institutions' level of academic qualifications	Full-time/ Part-time (No teaching hours per week) Years of teaching experience	Disciplinary areas	Occupational/ life experiences
A Female 40s P1	FE college level 5	Full-time 4 years	Radio production and journalism	Civil servant, information researcher and EFL teacher. Worked and lived in Japan
B Male 50s P1, 2	FE college level 5	Full-time over 3 years	Health and social care	Worked in the health and social care sector. NVQ assessor
C Male 40s P1	Adult and community level 5	Part-time (4 hrs/wk) 6 years	Art – painting and drawing	Architect and print maker

(*Continued*)

Table 7.1 (Continued)

Participant Gender Age Project participation	Teaching institutions' level of academic qualifications	Full-time/ Part-time (No teaching hours per week) Years of teaching experience	Disciplinary areas	Occupational/ life experiences
D Female 50s P1, 2	Dental hygiene institution level 4	Part-time (10 hrs/wk) 7 years	Dental hygiene, psychology and biology	Dental hygienist. Lived and worked abroad with the Navy (e.g. Malta)
E Male 50s P1	FE college level 5	Full-time 4 years (28 years including other education sectors)	Mathematics, physics and biology	Lived and worked in South Africa
F Female 30s P2	Adult and community level 4	Full-time 6 years	Life skills and IT	Lived abroad in her adolescence and had experienced homelessness and extreme poverty
G Female 50s P1, 2	Adult and community level 5	Part-time (4 hrs/wk) 20 years	Art – printmaking, textiles, drawing and painting	Worked as a community worker at a women's centre on art projects and for an under-fives project
H Female 30s P1, 2	Adult and community level 5	Part-time (5 hrs/wk) 5 years	Dance and Feldenkrais movement	Lived, studied and worked abroad
I Male 50s P1, 2	FE college level 5	Full-time 15 years	IT, art and palmistry	Graphic artist, homeopath, palmist and reflexologist. Worked and lived in Australia, Switzerland and the US

Discussion

The discussion is approached in two parts in order to consider the two issues posed in this chapter. The first part deals with the first issue, which is FE teaching knowledge from evidence-based research. The second part relates to the other issue, which is offering a collaborative and reflective peer-review approach to FE teacher training.

I will use the two most recent teaching standards to critique the current understanding of teacher knowledge in the training of FE teachers and from the findings of the first project, the import of teaching knowledge in the teacher education curriculum. The previous set of teaching standards by the former Further Education National Training Organisation (FENTO) (1999) included knowledge as one of the three themes, which were domain-wide knowledge (as applied to all areas of teaching, e.g. vocational and academic subject areas), generic knowledge (which related to each standard) and essential knowledge (which related to specific aspects of each standard). This document (FENTO, 1999) provided a prescriptive competence-based listing of such items from pages 5 to 41. It included the notion of three forms of teaching knowledge, which gave an import to teaching knowledge in a curriculum and thus might be used in teacher training. However, the sources and descriptions of such knowledge from research-based literature were not included. Significantly for this sector, teachers' occupational experiences were not viewed as relevant to the standards.

Coming to the teaching and training qualifications published by the former LSIS (2013b), it offers a slimmer document of thirty-eight pages with an emphasis on the learner over three levels with varying programme routes, including adult literacy and adult numeracy. This emphasis includes an expectation that a trainee teacher should link theory such as subject knowledge (including vocational-related areas) and pedagogic knowledge with practice and, learn from other practitioners. The document also recognizes trainee teacher's experiences and skills. As with the previous standard, it has references to teaching knowledge as well as no additional explanations about the sources, descriptions and applications of diverse teaching knowledge to teacher training. Despite the relevance of occupational experiences, little emphasis was given to this either as part of teaching knowledge or its role in a teacher's pedagogic activity. From the perspectives of the two recent standards, there appears to be a trend that has moved away from a prescriptive competence-related approach to become a pathway-based series of training programmes over three levels. Positively, both standards mention the need for research, professional development and collaboration.

To an extent, the aforementioned standards encompass knowledge types relating to Shulman's (1987) typology such as content knowledge, general pedagogical knowledge and Verloop *et al.'s* (2001) knowledge of learners with its focus on their learning. The standards also offer a nod to Loughran *et al.'s* 'Principles of teaching for quality learning' with the encouragement to learn from peers and an expectation that trainee teacher's biographical experiences are encouraged (Clandinin, 1985). Even teaching knowledge was included as part of the standards (Young, 2013).

Though there are implicit references to the 'typologists' group of literature sources, however, these are related mostly to the compulsory sectors, which are not necessarily specific to the FE sector. Drawing from the findings of the first project (Loo, 2012) and the earlier literature review, there is a need to explore and expand the typologies of teaching knowledge that are appropriate for FE. Some of the themes identified from this project have relevance to this chapter. One relates to the inclusion of occupational experiences of the trainee teachers, thus reflecting the distinctiveness of the FE sector and also giving legitimacy to this significant form of professional experience where it could be incorporated into the pedagogic activities of these trainee teachers in the teaching practices on vocational programmes. The other relevant themes from the project (Loo, 2012) are the opportunities for these teachers and other researchers to carry out research on areas such as teaching knowledge in the sector, disciplinary knowledge in relation to vocational areas and the sources and applications of diverse teaching knowledge to pedagogic activities in vocational courses. In short, the project found there should be a more evidence-based approach to teaching knowledge that is relevant to the FE sector.

The next part of this chapter uses findings from the second project (Loo, 2013) to highlight the lessons that may be applied to improve the quality of trainee teachers' pedagogic activities via a collaborative and reflective peer-review approach. These findings (as ascertained from the application of thematic and other forms of analysis indicated in the previous section), for the purposes of this chapter, revolve around three themes and they include the specificities of the socio-cultural-related, multi-modes of the session in question ('Taking History'); 'perceptions of reality'; and 'learning from peer review interaction beyond the digitally recorded session' (Loo, 2013). Collaboration in this context refers to the project participants discussing their digitally recorded teaching sessions in a peer-review environment using a multimodality framework (Kress, 2010). Reflective peer review relates to the constructive and supportive manner in which the discussions take place using the structured reflective approach (Pollard et al., 2008).

The remainder of this discussion uses the 'Taking History' digitally recorded session as a device to delineate the aims of this chapter. It was a simulated session of dental practice in the teaching institution, which consisted of partitioned-off cubicles for dental hygiene students to practice their clinical skills. Each cubicle was furnished with the relevant equipment such as a dental patient's chair, lighting and mouth wash facility. The aim of this session was for the students to practice taking the oral history of their 'patients' (who were their colleagues). The use of video recordings and interview demonstrated evidence of the ways in which pedagogic knowledge of learning activities can be developed through a reflective peer review as participant D in this project discovered:

> I was not aware of it until I watched it myself and particularly this time. These students were not paying attention to me; they were just thinking

what is going on in this other room where their colleagues were being examined. Gosh, this was something I have not realised if I did not watch that tape. This is a plus point of having the tape to play back.

(Participant D)

An advantage of this thematic approach ('perceptions of reality') of replaying the digitally recorded session was to allow Participant D additional time and space to reflect on the teaching group dynamics and the multi-modes of pedagogic activities. As indicated by Participant D's earlier quotation, she was not totally aware of the dynamics and pedagogic activities whilst she was 'in-situ'. An example of the group dynamics was the body language and the seeming lack of attentiveness of the students to Participant D's delivery before and after the entry of the student after her viva. During this exercise, the students in the session were empathetic towards one of their colleagues, who had to undergo a viva examination, and its result would impact her academic outcome. This replay also has the additional advantage for Participant D to discuss with her peers the 'specificities of the session' such as group dynamics (e.g. gaze, posture, facial expressions and voice of the students) and related pedagogic contexts. The replay also provides the trainee teachers/peers opportunities to discuss additional insights relating to her pedagogic activities. Therefore, the impact of a peer/tutor review of recorded teaching sessions may act as a useful tool for reflection and also afford greater understanding by means of critical observation and constructive discussion by the group members (Loo, 2013).

Turning to another theme, 'learning from peer observation beyond the digitally recorded session', it is useful to examine this interview comment from Participant I:

Use of [the digital] camcorder has the advantage of looking at how other teachers teach. The PGCE course did not allow that. At least in this [peer review] approach, one can look at how others do it and then discuss it. It offers a way of bench-marking, gives us more tools and also allows you to be yourself.

(Participant I)

The adoption of this approach offers opportunities to observe peers' pedagogic activities (LSIS, 2013b; Verloop *et al.*, 2001), which may inform and improve their teaching. This comparative approach needs to be tempered with the specific variations involving their peers in a reflective peer-review environment where such variations may include learners, programmes, teaching settings, regulations and the requirements of a related professional body (as in the case of the dental hygiene programme). Additionally, individual teacher's biographical experiences of occupation, life and pedagogy need to be factored in as indicated in such variations in Table 7.1 and as this participant suggested:

There is so much about the subtlety of teaching which you can't write about in great detail but [it is] much easier to look at it, like a [digitally recorded] session, and to discuss it.

(Participant G)

Participant G worked as a part-time art teacher at an FE college with previous work experiences as a community worker to learners of different ages. In the earlier quotation, she compared the similarities of an art discipline with teaching where a large degree of knowledge and activities could not be easily explicated. These tacit aspects of teaching chimed with Loughran *et al.*'s (2003) study, though not the occupation-related aspects. In this context, the previous point offers a new insight into Loughran's study of teaching knowledge in the compulsory sector. Participant G also indicated that it would be easier to demonstrate, use analogies and metaphors and to provide visual aids to assist in the understanding of this recorded teaching session. The next quotation on the tacit dimension of occupational teaching offers further insights into the training of teachers with occupational experiences:

> It is difficult to teach manual dexterity as you need to be like a detective by being able to look into somebody's mouth, describe what you see and be able to say why it is different and work [it] out provided they (the learners) have the theoretical knowledge and that they are able to apply it to the situation. There are transitional stages where the students can apply their theoretical knowledge, each of them to detect and identify deposits on the teeth and how to remove it and having the confidence to remove them. Students are afraid to harm the patient, which [is as] it should be but experienced tutors know the amount of pressure to use and perhaps the angle of applying the instrument. That [in] itself is quite hard to impart.
>
> (Teacher D)

Referring to Participant G's use of analogies and metaphors in vocational teaching in the earlier part of the reflective peer review session, Participant D used the analogy of washing up a mug in relation to brushing the inside and outside of one's teeth for dental hygiene purposes. Furthering this investigation of vocational teaching, the earlier quotation refers to the tacit aspects of teaching dental hygiene. One may ascertain three forms of knowledge are used in this kind of situation: disciplinary knowledge, occupational knowledge and the everyday knowledge and experiences of the learners. The disciplinary knowledge (Shulman, 1987; Verloop *et al.*, 2001; Young, 2013), in terms of dental hygiene, consists of relevant technical and scientific forms of knowledge. It is technical in the sense that knowledge is required by the learner in order to apply it to this session on 'Taking History'. Scientific knowledge is also required in the sciences such as anatomy, psychology and physiology, which had been covered in other teaching sessions. The occupational knowledge and experiences derived from the session, as inferred by Clandinin (1985) and explicated by Loo (2012), consisted of two aspects. The first was the support and guidance of the teacher using her occupational experience and knowledge/know-how, and the second aspect related to the learner's experience in a role play as patient and/or dental hygienist in a simulated environment and the use of the supporting clinical equipment, instruments and formalized dental record forms for taking a patient's oral history.

These teacher-and-student related occupational/professional experiences serve as a possible learning approach for becoming a professional dental hygienist. Relating to the previous part of this discussion, these forms of knowledge require further research in order to have a better understanding of this neglected area. The final type of knowledge relates to the everyday experiences (Bernstein, 1990; Loughran *et al.*, 2003) involving the learner's personal experiences of visiting a dental clinic and her/his awareness of the roles of being a dental hygienist.

In terms of how the three types of knowledge may be applied to the occupational teaching and learning in this simulated "Taking History' session, the vertical knowledge or disciplinary knowledge as subscribed by Bernstein (1990), Evans *et al.* (2010) and Young (2013) offers an entry point into the processes of recontextualisation. This can be the content of the dental hygiene curriculum where the relevant part of it was selected for this recorded session and where the related disciplinary source, e.g. anatomy was recontextualised for the purpose of dental hygiene. This process was termed by Evans *et al.* (2010) as 'content recontextualisation', and the choice of applying teaching strategies such as demonstration by the teacher and simulated practice by the learner to this session would be called 'pedagogic recontextualisation'. Bernstein and Young were of the view that the vertical/theoretical and the everyday/tacit aspects of knowledge would not be modified after the recontexualisation processes. However, others (Loo, 2012, 2014; Muller, 2014; Winch, 2010) suggest that the two forms of knowledge may be changed and integrated to an extent resulting from such recontextualisation processes. Loo (2014) referred to it as a form of 'ongoing recontextualisation' as it related to the application of disciplinary knowledge (e.g. anatomy) in a different disciplinary subject (i.e. dental hygiene) for the teacher and the learners in this specific simulated session. Referring to the earlier part of this discussion, further evidence-based research is needed surrounding the application of the forms of knowledge that occur in vocational settings. The mutability of the theoretical/vertical and the tacit/everyday forms of knowledge is further illustrated by the two quotations that follow:

> Teaching motivates me, gives me a sense of purpose and making a difference as well as informs my occupational practices, e.g. creation of an ideal home as a theme with students, parents and teachers as a way of managing art, architecture and teaching.
>
> (Teacher C)

> The transition from practice (as a dental hygienist) to teaching is easier if I practice regularly to keep my confidence level and speed up.
>
> (Teacher D)

As detailed in Table 7.1, Participant C was a practising print maker and architect alongside his part-time teaching in art in adult and community settings, and the background of Participant D was indicated earlier. The mutability of these teachers' disciplinary/vertical knowledge (of architecture and print making and anatomy and dental hygiene, respectively) alongside their pedagogic knowledge and their everyday/horizontal knowledge of life and related tacit experiences relating to life, occupational practice and teaching are intricately linked as part of ongoing recontextualisation processes. These processes may also suggest that there are symbiotic relationships (Loo, 2012) between occupational, teaching and life experiences as with Teacher C and occupational and teaching experiences with Teacher D. The final narrative by Teacher I offers another form of symbiotic relationship between pedagogic, occupational and biographical experiences:

> I've been a student and lecturer for the past ten years so my experiences have been on both sides of the fence and in homeopathy as a student and seeing how different teachers cope . . . invariably, my experiences as a teacher and as a student always apply in my teaching, as I am a perpetual student. My approach to teaching is not to use a big stick and not dumb down to primary and secondary levels but work on delivery and start from learners' world. I believe that my extensive life and work experience gained from living and working in Australia, Switzerland and the US as well as here in the UK has given me a tolerant and curiosity-focused approach to the education process.
> (Teacher I)

Teacher I, with his details recounted earlier, showed a more conventional symbiotic relationship, as investigated by Clandinin (1985), where his three forms of know-how included emotional and moralistic connections with his learners, which informed his visionary approach to teaching.

The use of the data, quantitative and qualitative, and the thematic analysis from the two projects described provide 'live' exemplars for this chapter to argue for an evidence-based and collaborative approach to the training of FE teachers with occupational experiences.

Insights and practical curriculum implications

This chapter offers a curriculum solution to the current under-developed and inconsistent approach to combining knowledge and experiences from the disciplines/occupations, pedagogy and life in order to train teachers who have occupational experiences. This approach draws on the empirical research findings of two projects. The chapter builds on the recognition of the importance of knowledge in the teacher education curriculum to call for more evidence-based research to understanding the complexity of occupational learning and teaching from the perspectives of its definition, sources and application. The chapter also offers a collaborative approach to facilitating teaching via reflective peer reviewing sessions of digitally recorded teaching sessions. In addition, it highlights the teachers' learning and teaching activities via the use of recontextualisation (and in particular ongoing recontextualisation) as means to understanding these complexities.

There are implications that arise for teachers, teaching institutions and policy makers. For teachers, this approach offers trainee teachers '360 degree' training opportunities of integrating their disciplinary and pedagogic knowledge with their reflective peer reviews. The call for further evidence-based findings of teaching knowledge highlights the importance of and gives credibility to occupational experiences as part of the complex nature of FE teaching knowledge. For teaching institutions, supportive structures would facilitate the teaching workforce to become informed professionals where research activities may enable them to become 'producers' and not mere consumers of pedagogic knowledge. The teacher education curriculum (of the current 120 credits programme and 15 credits system) may include an embedded focus on observations and recordings of real-life teaching sessions, supported by classroom sessions on theories, planning, etc. Furthermore, optional modules totalling forty-five credits may offer research knowledge and collaborative activities, opportunities to update occupational expertise and exploration of pedagogic strategies towards the improvement of occupational/vocational teaching and learning. For policy makers, the emphasis on knowledge content in the teacher training curricula and the support given to improve research opportunities would professionalise the teaching workforce and hopefully impact teaching quality and ultimately inspection outcomes.

Note

1 This chapter is based on the article, Loo, S. Y. (2014). Placing 'knowledge' in teacher education in the English further education teaching sector: An alternative approach based on collaboration and evidence based research. *British Journal of Educational Studies*, 62(3), 337–354.

References

Barnett, M. (2006) Vocational knowledge and vocational pedagogy, in M. Young and J. Gamble (eds.) *Knowledge, Curriculum and Qualifications for South African Further Education*. Cape Town: Human Sciences Research Council Press, pp. 143–158.

Bernstein, B. (1990) *The Structuring of Pedagogic Discourse: Class, Codes and Control*. London and New York: Routledge.

Clandinin, J. (1985) Personal practical knowledge: A study of teachers' classroom images. *Curriculum Inquiry*, 15(4), 361–385.

Cohen, L., Manion, L. and Morrison, K. (2000) *Research Methods in Education*. London: Routledge Falmer.

Department for Business, Innovation, Skills and Education (BIS). (2012a) *The Richard Review of Apprenticeships*. London: BIS.

Department for Business, Innovation and Skills (BIS). (2012b) *Professionalism in Further Education: Final Report of the Independent Review Panel*. London: BIS.

Department for Education (DfE). (2010) *The Importance of Teaching. Cm 7980*. London: The Stationery Office.

Department for Education (DfE). (2011) *Review of Vocational Education – The Wolf Report*. London: DFE.

Education and Training Foundation (ETF). (2014) *Professional Standards for Teachers and Trainers in England: Initial Guidance for Users*. London: ETF.

Evans, K., Guile, D., Harris, J. and Allan, H. (2010) Putting knowledge to work: A new approach. *Nurse Education Today*, 30(3), 245–251.

Frontier Economics Limited. (2014) *Further Education Workforce Data for England: Analysis of the 2012–2013 Staff Individualized Record Data.* London: Frontier Economics Limited.

Further Education National Training Organisation (FENTO). (1999) *Standards for Teaching and Supporting Learning in Further Education in England and Wales.* London: FENTO.

Kress, G. (2010) *Multimodality: A Social Semiotic Approach to Contemporary Communication.* London: Routledge.

Learning and Skills Improvement Service (LSIS). (2013a) *Commission on Adult Vocational Teaching and Learning.* Coventry: LSIS.

Learning and Skills Improvement Service (LSIS). (2013b) *Teaching and Training Qualifications for the Further Education and Skills Sector in England (2013): Guidance for Employers and Practitioners.* Coventry: LSIS.

Loo, S.Y. (2012) The application of pedagogic knowledge to teaching: A conceptual framework. *International Journal of Lifelong Education*, 31(6), 705–723.

Loo, S.Y. (2013) Professional development of teachers: Using multimodality and reflective peer review approaches to analyse digitally recorded teaching practices. *Teacher Development: An International Journal of Teachers' Professional Development*, 17(4), 499–517.

Loo, S.Y. (2014) Placing 'knowledge' in teacher education in the English further education sector: An alternative approach based on collaboration and evidence-based research. *British Journal of Educational Studies*, 62(3), 337–354.

Loughran, J., Mitchell, I. and Mitchell, J. (2003) Attempting to document teachers' professional knowledge. *Qualitative Studies in Education*, 16(6), 853–873.

Muller, J. (2014) Every picture tells a story: Epistemological access and knowledge. *Education as Change*, 18(2), 255–269.

Pollard, A., Anderson, J., Maddock, M., Swaffield, S., Warin, J. and Warwick, P. (2008) *Reflective Teaching: Evidence-Informed Professional Practice.* London: Continuum.

Shulman, L.S. (1987) Knowledge and teaching: Foundations of the new reform. *Harvard Educational Review*, 57(1), 1–22.

Tatto, M.T. (2013) Changing Trends in Teacher Education Policy and Practice: International perspectives and future challenges for educational research. *Research Intelligence*, 121, 16–17.

Verloop, N., Van Driel, J. and Meijer, P. (2001) Teacher knowledge and the knowledge base of teaching. *International Journal of Educational Research*, 35(5), 441–461.

Winch, C. (2010) *Dimensions of Expertise: A Conceptual Exploration of Vocational Education.* London: Continuum.

Young, M. (2013) Overcoming the crisis in curriculum theory: A knowledge-based approach. *Journal of Curriculum Studies*, 45(2), 101–118.

Section 3
Pedagogy

8 "It's all about work"
New times, post-Fordism and vocational pedagogy

James Avis

Introduction

This chapter[1] brings together two sets of arguments. The first addresses constructions of western economies that suggest there is something potentially progressive in knowledge-based economies (KBEs). The second related set of arguments considers the manner in which we make sense of vocational pedagogy. This may be understood in either an expansive or restrictive manner, which in turn articulates with conceptualisations of KBEs and the role of vocational education and training (VET) in developing a creative and innovative workforce. Whilst the following discussion draws largely on the English experience, it has a wider purchase, addressing globalisation, capitalism in its various forms, social democracy and neo-liberalism, as well as the purpose of vocational pedagogy. Consequently, it engages with European Union concerns with the development of knowledge-based economies (EU, 2002, 2010). In European policy space and especially in countries such as Germany, VET addresses questions of citizenship and democratic participation (Coffield & Williamson, 2011; Winch, 2012), whereas in England it has a narrower remit more tightly rooted in neo-liberalism, with an instrumental focus on the immediacy of waged labour. In the latter case, this is out of step with the presumed demands of KBEs for the development of the innovative and creative capacity of labour.

The starting point for this chapter derives from two related sources: the Compass Education Group's[2] (2015) *Big Education: Learning for the 21st Century*, and Spours's (2014) "Education, the Economy and the State in 'New Times'". Spours, who was involved in writing both documents, drew on notions derived from the 'New Times' debate of the late 1980s and '90s, linking it to the current conjuncture and particularly to discussions about Labour party policy. The 'New Times' project suggested that post-Fordism represented an epochal change and that older Fordist conceptualisations of social, economic and political processes were less than helpful. This project was closely associated with *Marxism Today* and in particular its special issue on 'New Times' published in October 1988. The notion of 'New Times' can be linked to the decline of industrial capitalism in the West and the increasing significance attached to post-Fordism. Drawing upon this analysis, Spours argued that "New Times is a 'subordinate progressive trend' within 'regressive neo-liberalism' to be shaped and built" (2014: 4). That is to say, within 'New Times' there are two potentially contradictory futures, both of which derive from the new technological, organisational and social environment facing society. On the one hand, this may facilitate the development of a social formation that is more egalitarian and democratic, in which "people will increasingly have the opportunity to collaborate, co-operate, share, experiment, learn, fail and try again together. In these new networks, power and decision making can be the property of us all. And on these emerging flat planes where everyone's voice counts, everyone can be heard and anyone can know anything anywhere; the key skills of the future will be relational, emotional and empathetic" (Compass, 2015: 12).

Simultaneously, on the other hand, this new environment may be appropriated by 'big business' to serve its interests and become wedded to a neo-liberal state that validates cultures of individualism and competitiveness. Importantly, and, as with the earlier argument, at the same time, 'New Times' is thought to hold progressive possibilities that extend beyond the confines of Fordism and a restrictive neo-liberalism.

In the following, I revisit some of the earlier arguments surrounding the 'New Times' debate and post-Fordism, as this has an affinity with and is applicable to current discussions about innovation, creativity and the increased importance attached to KBEs. There are a set of arguments that examine KBEs, suggesting these contain radical if not transformative possibilities. This derives from two of the features of post-Fordism. First, the importance attached to creativity and, second, the contribution of workers to the success of the organisation. The nature of the firm as well as the manner in which surplus value is created has undergone a number of significant changes. Various notions are drawn upon to illustrate these that have not only affected individual firms but also the wider economy. Thus we encounter a number of conceptualisations such as mass customisation, co-configuration, social production, co-opetition, produsers, 'playbor', Pro-ams,[3] P2P (peer-to peer), open source and so on. All of these terms, in their different ways, suggest that erstwhile dichotomies have broken down, that is to say the division between consumer and producers has become blurred, with consumers also contributing to production. Immaterial labour that draws upon the intellectual capacity of those in and out of waged labour has become significant in facilitating innovation and the generation of surplus value.

It has become something of a commonplace for those on the left to argue that the concern with competitiveness is predicated upon a number of ideological distortions. This is the 'worst of times' marked by a 'regressive neo-liberalism' that Spours (2014) and the Compass Group (2015) describe. Key amongst the ideological distortions embedded within neo-liberalism are the presumption of upskilling; the increased salience of knowledge work, that is to say value-added waged labour; and the promise of a steadily increasing standard of living and well-being, all premised on the development of a globally competitive economy. The state's concern with competitiveness is located within neo-liberalism, with its tendency towards individualisation, the precariousness of waged labour and, for the majority of workers, a secular decline in wages and allied benefits (Any on; Blacker, 2013; Brown *et al.*, 2011; Dorling, 2014: Jin *et al.*, 2011; Marsh, 2011).

Post-Fordism

A note of caution. I am using the term post-Fordism to describe a particular current of thought present in the 1990s that pointed towards the transformation of waged work, specifically in England, but also in western economies. This understanding of post-Fordist imagery can be contrasted with analyses that view it as a particular stage of capitalist development. The focus here is on post-Fordism as an ideology, and the contrast that can be made between it and Fordism with respect to the economy, competition, the production process and labour. Brown and Lauder's (1992, Table 1.1 p. 4) illustrate a particular model of the shift from Fordism to post-Fordism. Fordist production processes sit alongside Keynesian Welfarism and feature protected national markets, mass production of standardised products, bureaucratic organisational structures with competition based on economies of scale that seek to maximise capacity and reduce cost. This is contrasted with post-Fordism, which mobilises a rather different logic and sits comfortably with KBEs. In this instance, competition is global, based on innovation and the development of flexible production systems that respond rapidly to market changes and organisational structures that are flatter and marked by distributed leadership.

This description of post-Fordism offers a number of familiar themes that continue to resonate some twenty years on, that is to say notions of flexible production, flatter and responsive organisational structures, with the need for continual innovation to secure competitive advantage. These ideas are reflected in Spours's (2014) work and his description of 'New Times'.

New times – technological, economic and social

- New Times is a global phenomenon comprising

    - Technological and digital revolution
    - Flexible production (post-Fordism)
    - Lateral communication – social networking; blogging
    - New forms of organisation – flatter companies
    - The social economy

- New Times is a 'subordinate progressive trend' within 'regressive neo-liberalism' to be shaped and built (Spours, 2014: 4)

For Spours, these developments have arisen out of the growth of digital technologies that have been facilitated by the increasing salience of social and interactive networks. In a not dissimilar fashion, Araya cites four features of digital capitalism (2013: 27).

Four features of digital capitalism

1. The diffusion of information and communication technologies (ICTs) and consequent transformations in Fordist production
2. The growing significance of a global market and globally fragmented production systems

3   The increased importance of highly educated workers or human capital within continuous cycles of creative innovation
4   The rise of alternative centres of production and consumption outside advanced industrialized countries

(Araya, 2013: 27)

Araya's description aligns with KBEs and their emphases on innovation, creativity and the development of human capital – the increased importance attached to immaterial/intellectual labour. This again reflects the shift from Fordism to post-Fordism and its impact on the labour process (Brown & Lauder, 1992, Table 1.1 p. 4). This is reflected in the shift from the detailed division of labour towards one marked by the growth of flexible specialisation and multi-skilling. Consequently, workers engage in high-skilled, high-trust labour which requires regular on-the-job training with a premium being attached to the 'knowledgeable' worker. The predictability that was a feature of Fordist labour markets has been superseded by turbulence set within conditions of economic and technological uncertainty.

In the 1980s and '90s, a number of writers felt that these post-Fordist changes presaged progressive possibilities (Brown & Lauder, 1992). This potential derived from the importance placed upon the 'knowledgeable worker', who was required to mobilise skills and discretion in the workplace. Keep and James capture the ideological tenor of such arguments when they write

> [a] 'knowledge-driven economy' that would usher in an era of unbridled creativity where a workforce of knowledge workers, would command 'authorship' over their own work routines and activities, would be created.
>
> (Keep & James, 2012: 211)

We can see these themes reflected in current discussions which emphasise the importance of lateral communication, social networking and blogging, as well as the social economy which Spours (2014) has discussed. These changes have been facilitated by "the diffusion of information and communication technologies and the consequent transformations in Fordist production" (Araya, 2013: 27). In addition, such workplace practices are thought to be located in organisations having flatter and more flexible structures.

Conceptualisations of portfolio working (Handy, 1990) and distributed leadership (Harris, 2008) capture some of these ideas, as do the more radical notions of collective intelligence (Lacey, 1988) and connectivity (Young, 1993, 1998). It was these latter currents that were thought to carry progressive possibilities presaging the transformation of work relations. So, for example Brown and Lauder (1992) cite Lacey's work approvingly.

Skills and talents are concerned with solving problems within already existing paradigms and systems of knowledge. Intelligence has to do with understanding the relationship between complex systems and making judgments about when it is appropriate to work within existing paradigms and when it is appropriate to create new courses of action or avenues of thought.... "**Collective intelligence** [is] defined as a measure of our ability to face up to problems that confront us collectively and to develop collective solutions" (my emphasis; Lacey, 1988: 93–94).

The point is that the transition from Fordist to post-Fordist work relations was thought to open up such possibilities. The development of collective intelligence anticipated more egalitarian and democratic relations in much the same way as is the case with current versions of 'New Times'.

> 'the best of times' – in which people will increasingly have the opportunity to collaborate, co-operate, share, experiment, learn, fail and try again together. In these new networks, power and decision-making can be the property of us all. And on these emerging flat planes where everyone's voice counts, everyone can be heard and anyone can know anything anywhere, the key skills of the future will be relational, emotional and empathetic.
> (Compass, 2015: 12)

Notions of transition and progressive possibilities were also a feature of Young's work in the 1990s. Here the notion of connectivity not only served an economic but also an educational purpose that heralded the possibility of enhanced democratisation. The point is that there appear to be a range of arguments that seek to wrest progressive possibilities from the 'New Times' debate in both its early and later manifestations. Young wrote the following about connectivity:

> Connective specialisation is concerned with the links between combinations of knowledge and skills in the curriculum and wider democratic and social goals. At the individual level it refers to the need for an understanding of the social, cultural, political and economic implications of any knowledge or skill in its context, and how, through such a concept of education, an individual can learn both specific skills and knowledge and the capacity to take initiatives, whatever their specific occupation or position ... As a definition of educational purpose it aims to transcend the traditional dichotomy of the 'educated person' and the 'competent employee' which define the purpose of the two tracks of the divided curriculum.
> (Young, 1993: 218)

Interestingly, this argument draws together notions of the educated person and the competent employee in much the same way as in the current version of this debate. Both versions imply that there are at least two variants of capitalism, one marked by the perversities of neo-liberalism and the other, a more human, developmental and progressive form offering the possibility of non-alienating labour where our species being can be expressed. The preceding has a bearing upon the way in which we could think about vocational pedagogy and its educative as well as progressive possibilities. This is particularly the case if the historical movement is towards post-Fordist work relations or, in Compass Education Group's terms, "the best of times".

However, during the 1990s, it became apparent that the optimism surrounding these constructions of post-Fordism were and continue to be illusionary. Flexibilisation, adaptability and insecurity have become features of working life with such processes being linked to individualisation, responsibilisation, precariousness and neo-Fordism. In 1996, Brown and Lauder pointed out the following:

> Neo-Fordism can be characterised in terms of creating greater market flexibility through a reduction in social overheads and the power of trade unions, the privatisation of public utilities and the welfare state, as well as a celebration of competitive individualism.
>
> (Brown & Lauder, 1992: 5)

Neo-Fordism reflects what the Compass Education Group refer to as the 'worst of times'. Brown *et al.'s* (2011) more recent work on the US is much less sanguine than their earlier writing, with its argument equally applicable to other western economies. In contradistinction to post-Fordist imagery, they argue that the income of workers has become increasingly vulnerable. They point towards the collapse of the post-war opportunity structure in which the possibility of upwards mobility was significant together with a continually improving standard of living and the expectation that children would be better off than their parents (Allen & Ainley, 2014). For Brown *et al.* (2011), knowledge workers encounter digital Taylorism, which has been facilitated by the development of information and communication technologies. Digital Taylorism refers to the way in which new digital technologies enable formerly skilled knowledge work to be standardised. This argument resonates with Marx (1976) and Braverman (1974), who suggest that capitalism contains a logic towards the deskilling of labour and its immiseration. Alongside these processes, Brown *et al.* point towards the possibility of a high-skill, low-wage nexus for workers in the West. They argue that amongst knowledge workers there is a polarisation between those experiencing digital Taylorism and a small elite who are deemed to possess the skills, creativity and talent that enable transnational companies to outperform their competitors. These workers receive a wage premium which can be seen as a feature of Brown *et al.'s* (2008) global 'war for talent'.

The reason for re-visiting these earlier discussions (and see Avis, 2010, 2013a, 2013b, 2016) is that they are as relevant today as they were in the 1980s and '90s. However, I would like to make two additional observations. The first concerns Spours's claim that "New Times is a 'subordinate progressive trend' within 'regressive neo-liberalism' to be shaped and built" (2014: 4). This could be seen as a call for action, a site of struggle, but it is also set within a contradictory location. After all, capital is not all of a piece, and post-Fordist imagery alongside 'New Times', whilst offering certain benefits, is nevertheless set on a capitalist terrain. Post-Fordism addresses the concerns of a particular fraction of capital that coexists alongside other forms. At best, 'New Times' and post-Fordism could be framed within a social democratic politics that is limited by its failure to develop a robust anti-capitalist project. It is important to recall that in a context of digital Taylorism, the hype surrounding KBE's demand for creative and innovative labour is deeply misleading. This hype can be seen as a fiction perpetuated by intellectuals who have aligned themselves with a modernised and progressive capitalism (Hutton, 2010; Sainsbury, 2013) that sets itself against neo-liberalism and, though allegedly more humane, is equally concerned with the extraction of surplus value.

The second and related point is that for some writers, post-Fordism and beyond represents changes in the mode of production, that is to say, the decline of industrial capitalism in the West and concomitant changes in the way capitalist organisations are understood. Thus we encounter conceptualisations of mass customisation, co-configuration, social production, produsers, and a number of similar terms, all of which emphasise the integration of consumers into the production process. These notions can be seen in Engeström's (2010) discussion of the historical modes of production in which social production anticipates the incipient socialisation of the means of production. In this he draws on the work of Marx as well as that of Victor and Boynton (1998). Whilst the shifts described will be uneven, there is, nevertheless, a trajectory in the direction of social production which goes beyond firm-based models of production. In this context, Engeström refers to Benkler's (2006) work on P2P, open source and social production, and in these instances, surplus value is generated by those external to the capitalist organisation and who provide free labour. This latter theme is addressed in a rather different and less sanguine understanding of current conditions in cognitive capitalism and Italian Workerism.

Cognitive capitalism

Gorz (2010), with others, suggests that industrial capitalism represents a particular stage of capitalist development and has been transcended by cognitive or immaterial capitalism (Boutang, 2011). Here surplus value is appropriate in a qualitatively different manner to the preceding stage. Marazzi, echoing the Compass Group's (2014: 12) rather more benign description of relational, emotional and empathetic skills, suggests,

> one's entire life is put to work, when knowledges and cognitive competences of the workforce (the general intellect that Marx spoke about in his Grundrisse) assume the role played by machines in the Fordist period, incarnated in the living productive bodies of cooperation, in which language, effects, emotions and relational and communication capacities all contributed to the creation of value.
>
> (2011: 113)

For those who adopt this argument, the knowledge and competences of the workforce are developed collectively by living labour, external to capitalist relations. This potential has arisen as a consequence of Fordism and Welfarism with Vercellone (2008) referring to "the constitution of a diffuse intellectuality generated by the development of mass education". He also argues that the social struggles that secured "the spread of social income and welfare services" resulted in conditions favourable to the development of knowledge-based economies.

The significance of this argument is that it prioritises the development of knowledge and views this as a collective and implicitly democratic accomplishment that occurs outside the direct control of capital with surplus value being appropriated in a qualitatively different manner to that found within industrial capitalism. There are resonances here with feminist analyses of housework, which examined the significance of unwaged labour for capitalist processes (Federici, 2012; Fortunati, 1995). This type of analysis also raises questions about vocational pedagogy. If, through labour that takes place external to the capitalist firm, we generate surplus value, this implies that 'life' itself is a vocational pedagogy. Whilst I do not want to exaggerate this, it has implications for the way in which we think about vocational education and pedagogy, especially in a context that stresses the need for adaptability and flexibility and where we are frequently 'produser' as well as part of the precariat.

Vocational education/pedagogy

Billett's (2005) research on vocational learning sets much of this in the workplace. By acknowledging this as a site of learning, we are able to dignify forms of labour that have been overlooked and often seen as demeaning. By recognising and credentialising this type of learning, a social justice agenda is addressed. Fuller and Unwin (2003), on a slightly different tack, explore workplace learning cultures for their pedagogic possibilities, arguing that these may be more or less restrictive or expansive. The former effectively mirrors Fordist and the latter post-Fordist work relations (see Evans *et al.*, 2006, fig 3.2 p. 61). There are several points to make about restrictive and expansive learning cultures and environments. The restrictive is set within a managerialist, performative and Taylorist/Fordist context and readily opens itself up to critique. This sits with critiques of performativity and audit culture that suggest these preclude the creative engagement of workers. In a sense, the restrictive is construed as anti-educative and subject to the critique of Fordist and Taylorist work relations – it is easy enough to rail against an impoverished Fordism. Expansive learning cultures are concerned with the development of variable labour power and represent a type of vocational pedagogy that is firmly set on a capitalist terrain. Such a stance is not so far from the view expressed by the Commission on Adult Vocational Teaching and Learning (CAVTL) who suggest

> the best vocational teaching and learning combines theoretical knowledge from the underpinning disciplines (for example, maths, psychology, human sciences, economics) with the occupational knowledge of practice (for example, how to cut hair, build circuit boards, administer medicines). To do this, teachers, trainers and learners have to recontextualise theoretical and occupational knowledge to suit specific situations. Both types of knowledge

are highly dynamic. So individuals need to carry on learning through being exposed to new forms of knowledge and practice in order to make real the line of sight to work.

(CAVTL, 2013: 15)

Paradoxically, CAVTL's position whilst appearing progressive reflects a somewhat restrictive model of VET, as it is preoccupied with a clear line of sight to work. Such an orientation can very easily lead to a narrow focus on the needs of employers and, to the extent that creativity and innovation are encouraged and valued, this is on the basis that it contributes to successful workplace practices. Critique is to be encouraged, provided it rests within this terrain and is 'business facing'. This understanding of vocational education/pedagogy simply refers to learning for work and developing the skills required to labour effectively. However, this is a peculiarly Anglo-Saxon conceptualisation of vocational education and pedagogy. Clarke and Winch (2007) suggest that it is thought of quite differently in other social formations. Whilst in the Anglo-Saxon world it is viewed as preparation for working life – a process of a rather technical and practical nature; in other societies, it can also encompass civic and academic education. It is often viewed as being as much concerned with personal development as it is with the needs of employers. In addition, it has been linked with identity formation as well as nation building. It is important to acknowledge that these additional features may be undercut by neo-liberalism. Vocational education and its pedagogy is inevitably marked by history and the society in which it is located, being shaped by the struggle between capital and labour as well as the balance of power and the concessions that have been won or lost. Progressive forms of VET may reflect the compromises made between capital and labour, but they may also be rhetorical and deeply ideological and justify situations where "one's entire life is put to work" (Marazzi, 2011: 113).

There are numerous models of vocational education and pedagogy that encompass notions of competence and socially situated workplace processes, as well as various conceptualisations of expansive learning as found in Engeström (2010) and Fuller and Unwin's work (2003; Evans *et al.*, 2006). Notwithstanding their differences, they all prioritise waged labour, even in the case of those that go beyond notions of expansive learning and allied cultures towards democratic participation and citizenship that are wedded to consensual or pluralistic models of society. In these cases, the antagonism between labour and capital are thought to be manageable. This position can also be found in accounts that discuss academic disciplinary knowledge and argue this is central to a social justice agenda. In this case, writers such as Wheelahan (2010) suggest that access to such knowledge is an element of distributed justice with this arising in several ways. Vocational education and pedagogy need to provide learners with the facility to evaluate and judge the claims made by academic disciplines. This potential will enable learners to critique disciplinary claims, albeit in a rudimentary fashion. In addition, disciplinary knowledge provides access to what Young (1998, 2008)) describes as 'powerful knowledge' in that it offers 'epistemic gains' that are not readily accessible in other forms of knowledge. However, such a position needs to be supplemented with what Johnson has described as "really useful knowledge":

> A knowledge of everyday circumstances, including a knowledge of why you were poor, why you were politically oppressed and why through the force of social circumstance, you were the kind of person you were, your character misshapen by a cruel competitive world.
>
> (Education Group, 1981: 37)

Although this goes beyond the claimed objectivity and validation of disciplinary knowledge by its community of scholars, it does seek to wrest a progressive politics from this and thereby engages in a politics of hope. In other words, the epistemic gains that derive from disciplinary knowledge can only take us so far and need to be mobilised politically in order to serve a social justice agenda.

Towards a conclusion

The 'New Times' anticipated by post-Fordism, together with calls for expansive forms of vocational education and pedagogy, hold progressive possibilities. However, the preceding argument suggests that this connection can be overstated. This can be seen in the work of those writers who argue that the 'New Times' offer the potential to transcend the perversities of neo-liberalism. Whilst this is undoubtedly the case, it is also important to recognise that this argument is constrained by the capitalist relations in which it is located. Capitalism is not all of a piece, and whilst 'New Times' emphasises the significance of knowledge work and immaterial labour, these are as deeply embedded in capital/labour relations as are other forms of work that coexist with these. Research associated with cognitive capitalism illustrates the way in which living labour contributes to the generation of surplus value. This in turn implies that our cultural and social lives that occur external to the capitalist organisation can be conceived of as a type of vocational pedagogy.

A more general discussion of vocational education and pedagogy raises questions about its expansive potential. Much of this debate is closely tied to the workplace and, unsurprisingly, is concerned with the development of variable labour power – in effect a conservative politics. This arises in spite of its commitment to social justice, yet as with 'New Times', there resides a progressive possibility. This derives from its engagement with the epistemic gains proffered by academic disciplines accompanied by a concern with really useful knowledge. This is a politics of hope that draws upon lived experience and that mobilises disciplinary knowledge as a resource in the struggle for social justice in an attempt to move beyond capitalism.

Notes

1 This chapter draws on arguments and develops those first presented in Avis, 2010, 2013a, b, 2016.
2 Compass originated as a pressure group that sought to influence policies of the UK Labour Party. It is committed to the development of a 'good' society in which equality, sustainability and democracy become a living reality. Compass now believes

"It's all about work" 103

that no single issue, organisation or political party can attain its goals and that, therefore, it needs to work and build alliances with a variety of groups. Spours convened the Compass Education Group (2015) and wrote much of its report.
3 "Produsers" (user-led production of content); "playbor" (a hybrid term for the blurring of 'play' and 'labour' on the internet); Pro-ams (a mixture of professional and amateur).

References

Allen, M. and Ainley, P. (2014) A New Direction for Vocational Learning or A Great Training Robbery? Initial Research into and Analysis of The Reinvention of Apprenticeships at The Start of the 21st Century, paper presented HIVE ESRC Seminar 28 February at the University of Greenwich.

Anyon, J. (2005) *Radical Possibilities: Public Policy, Urban Education and a New Social Movement.* New York: Routledge.

Araya, D. (2013) Education as transformation: Post-industrialization and the challenge of continuous innovation, in M.A. Peters, T. Besley and D. Araya (eds.) *The New Development Paradigm: Education, Knowledge Economy and Digital Futures.* New York: Peter Lang, pp. 19–34.

Avis, J. (2010) Workplace learning, knowledge, practice and transformation. *Journal for Critical Education Policy Studies*, 8(2) December 2010, 165–193. http://www.jceps.com/?pageID=article&articleID=197.

Avis, J. (2013a) Post-fordist illusions – Knowledge-based economies and transformation. *Power and Education*, 5(1), 16–27.

Avis, J. (2013b) Engeström's version of activity theory: A conservative praxis? in D. Scott (ed.) *Theories of Learning*, Vol 3. London: Sage, pp. 133–152.

Avis, J. (2016) *Social Justice, Transformation and Knowledge: Policy, Workplace Learning and Skills.* London: Routledge.

Benkler, Y. (2006) *The Wealth of Networks: How Social Production Transforms Markets and Freedom.* New Haven: Yale University Press.

Billett, S. (2005) Recognition of learning through work, in N. Bascia, A. Cumming, A. Datnow, K. Leithwood and D. Livingstone (eds.) *International Handbook of Educational Policy*. Dordrecht: The Netherlands Springer, pp. 943–962.

Blacker, D. (2013) *The Falling Rate of Learning and the Neoliberal Endgame.* Winchester: Zero Books.

Boutang, Y.M. (2011). *Cognitive Capitalism.* Cambridge: Polity.

Braverman, H. (1974) *Labor and Monopoly Capital: The Degradation of Work in the Twentieth Century.* New York: Monthly Review Press.

Brown, P. and Lauder, H. (eds.) (1992) *Education for Economic Survival: From Fordism to Post-Fordism.* London: Routledge.

Brown, P., Lauder, H. and Ashton, D. (2008) Education, globalisation and the future of the knowledge economy. *European Educational Research Journal*, 7(2), 131–56.

Brown, P., Lauder, H. and Ashton, D. (2011) *The Global Auction.* Oxford: Oxford University Press.

CAVTL. (2013) It's about work . . . Excellent adult vocational teaching and learning: The summary report of the commission on adult vocational teaching and learning. *Coventry LSIS*. http://www.excellencegateway.org.uk/content/eg5937 (Accessed 6 November 2013).

Clarke, L. and Winch, C. (2007) Introduction, in L. Clarke and C. Winch (eds.) *Vocational Education*. London: Routledge, pp. 1–18.

Coffield, F. and Williamson, B. (2011) *From Exam Factories to Communities of Discovery: The Democratic Route*. London: Bedford Way Papers.
Compass Education Group (2015) *Big Education: Learning for the 21st Century*. London: Compass. http://www.compassonline.org.uk/wp-content/uploads/2015/03/Compass-BIG-Education-DIGITAL-Final.pdf (Accesses 6 August 2015).
Dorling, D. (2014) *Inequality and the 1%*. London: Verso.
Education Group CCCS (1981) *Unpopular Education*. London: Hutchinson.
Engeström, Y. (2010) *From Teams to Knots: Activity-Theoretical Studies of Collaboration and Learning at Work*. Cambridge: Cambridge University Press, paperback edition.
European Union. (2002) The Copenhagen declaration, declaration of the European Ministers of vocational education and training and the European commission, convened in Copenhagen on 29 and 30 November on enhanced European cooperation in vocational education and training. http://ec.europa.eu/education/pdf/doc125_en.pdf (Accessed 1 January 2012).
European Union. (2010) The Bruges Communiqué on enhanced European cooperation in vocational education and training for the period 2011–2020. http://ec.europa.eu/education/lifelong-learning-policy/doc/vocational/bruges_en.pdf (Accessed 1 January 2012).
Evans, K., Hodkinson, P., Rainbird, H. and Unwin, L. (2006) *Improving Workplace Learning*. London: Routledge.
Federici, S. (2012) *Revolution at Point Zero*. Oakland: PM Press.
Fortunati, L. (1995) *The Arcane of Reproduction*. New York: Autonomedia.
Fuller, A. and Unwin, L. (2003) Learning as apprentices in the contemporary UK workplace: Creating and managing expansive and restrictive participation. *Journal of Education and Work*, 16(4), 407–426.
Gorz, A. (2010) *The Immaterial*. London: Seagull.
Handy, C. (1990) *The Age of Unreason*. London: Arrow.
Harris, A. (2008) *Distributed School Leadership*. London: Routledge.
Hutton, W. (2010) *Them and Us*. London: Little Brown.
Jin, W., Joyce, R., Phillips, D. and Sibieta, L. (2011) Poverty and inequality in the UK: 2011 IFS commentary C118. Joseph Rowntree Foundation. http://www.ifs.org.uk/comms/comm118.pdf (Accessed 20 November 2012).
Keep, E. and James, S. (2012) A Bermuda triangle of policy? 'Bad jobs', skills policy and incentives to learn at the bottom end of the labour market. *Journal of Education Policy*, 27(2), 211–230. http://dx.doi.org/10.1080/02680939.2011.595510.
Lacey, C. (1988) The idea of a socialist education, in H. Lauder and P. Brown (eds.) *Education in Search of a Future*. London: Falmer Press, pp. 91–98.
Marazzi, C. (2011) *The Violence of Financial Capitalism*. Los Angeles: Semiotext(e).
Marsh, J. (2011) *Class Dismissed*. New York: Monthly Review Press.
Marx, K. (1976) [1867] *Capital Volume 1*. Penguin: Harmondsworth.
Sainsbury, D. (2013) *Progressive Capitalism*. London: Biteback Publishing.
Spours, K. (2014) Education, the economy and the state in 'New Times', paper presented Post-Compulsory and Lifelong Learning SIG Seminar Series 2014, Vocational education and training: Policy, pedagogy and research, 27 January, Institute of Education, London.
Vercellone, C. (2008) *The New Articulation of Wages, Rent and Profit in Cognitive Capitalism*. Paris: Centre d'economie de la Sorbonne.
Victor, B. and Boynton, A.C. (1998) *Invented Here*. Boston: Harvard Business School Press.
Wheelahan, L. (2010) *Why Knowledge Matters in Curriculum*. London: Routledge.

Winch, C. (2012) *Dimensions of Expertise*. London: Continuum.
Young, M. (1993) A curriculum for the 21st century: Towards a new basis for overcoming the academic/vocational divisions. *British Journal of Educational Studies*, 41(3), 203–222.
Young, M. (1998) *The Curriculum of the Future: From the 'New Sociology of Education' to a Critical Theory of Learning*. London: Falmer
Young, M. (2008) *Bringing Knowledge Back in*. London: Routledge.

9 Constructions of knowledge through practice in general vocational education in England

Ann-Marie Bathmaker

Introduction

General vocational education for young people has been overshadowed by high-profile policy interest in apprenticeship and participation in higher education (HE) in England under recent governments. Nevertheless, though not at the centre of public attention, the quality, content and purpose of vocational education has been subject to major national review and reform in the past five years. In 2011, *The Wolf Report* was published. Its purpose was 'to consider how we can improve vocational education for 14–19 year olds and thereby promote successful progression into the labour market and into higher-level education and training routes' (Wolf, 2011: 19). In 2015, the UK's Department of Business, Innovation and Skills announced that the 'technical and professional education revolution continues', with plans to introduce twenty new professional and technical routes, following a review led by Lord Sainsbury reporting in 2016.[1] These reviews draw attention to the question of what knowledge should form part of general vocational qualifications and how it is decided. This chapter looks at this question by examining how knowledge is constructed in and through the practices of teaching and learning in general vocational education in England. The term general vocational education is used to refer to qualifications that are associated with a broad vocational area that are intended to be applied or practice oriented, but which primarily take place in educational settings.

The chapter is based on the Knowledge in Vocational Education project, a one-year research project (2010–11) funded by Edexcel, one of the main qualifications awarding bodies in England. The aim of the project was to investigate what is meant by 'knowledge' in general vocational education qualifications in England, who defines knowledge in this context, and how this is translated into practice. The project involved two phases. The first phase focused on the role of stakeholders in defining knowledge in general vocational education at levels 2 and 3 (equivalent to levels 4 and 5 in the European qualifications framework), while the second phase examined how teachers construct knowledge and translate their constructions into everyday teaching and learning practices. A previous paper based on phase 1 of the project showed how there was confusion amongst a range of different stakeholders over what constituted knowledge in general vocational qualifications and who defines it (Bathmaker, 2013). This chapter is based on phase 2 of the project and considers how the recontextualisation of knowledge through the practices of teaching and learning contributes to constructions of knowledge (Evans et al., 2010), and it is strongly influenced by perceptions of the needs and capabilities of the students participating in these pathways.

The growth of general vocational education in England

In 2013–14, legislation to raise the participation age was introduced in England so that from September 2016, all young people must continue in some form of education or training until at least their eighteenth birthday. The most recent data available at the time of this writing shows that by the end of 2013, 85.4 per cent of 16–18 year olds were already in education or training, and 69.9 per cent of these young people were in full-time education, while only 5.9 per cent were in work-based training (DfE, 2015).[2] There are no straightforward data that indicate what proportion of these young people follow general vocational education routes. However, data from the Higher Education Funding Council for England (HEFCE, 2015) show that out of a total of 253,595 students who were following either an academic A-level programme or a vocationally related BTEC programme[3] in 2012–13, nearly 20 per cent were taking a BTEC as their main qualification (205, 170 students were taking A-levels, compared with 48,425 taking BTEC qualifications). Based on these numbers, general vocational routes clearly play an important role in the provision of education and training for 16–18 year-olds, and their importance may increase rather than diminish with the raising of the participation age.

The present rates of participation are the culmination of increased staying on in post compulsory education in England since the late 1970s, with an expansion of participation in a range of general vocational education routes, which have run alongside vocational training schemes, offered in the workplace or by training providers. Successive general vocational qualifications have replaced one another since that time, as shown in Table 9.1.

Increased staying on and raising of the participation age might be seen as opening up education and training opportunities for all. However, expansion at the end of the 1970s coincided with reductions in youth employment, and there has been a continuing tension in the perceived role of general vocational routes and qualifications, with suggestions that they are at best a second-chance opportunity for lower achievers, who are not deemed capable of academic achievement, and at worst, a means of warehousing young people when employment is unavailable (see Banks et al., 1992; Bates, 1984; Bates & Riseborough, 1993).

Qualifications such as the Certificate in Pre-Vocational Education were explicitly 'prevocational ', implying that young people following these qualifications

Table 9.1 General vocational qualifications in England 1970s–2010s

Year	Qualification
1970s	Certificate of Further Education
1985	Certificate in Pre-Vocational Education (CPVE)
	One year post-16 course for students who might have gone on to apprenticeships before the recession and now stayed on in education rather than going on to the Youth Training Scheme
1980s	Diploma in Vocational Education. Replaced CPVE
1983	BTEC First Certificates and BTEC Diplomas
	The Business and Technician Education Council was formed in 1983 and offered full-time as well as part-time BTEC courses. BTECs have survived the wider changes to qualifications
1992	General National Vocational Qualifications (GNVQs)
	Introduced as a bridge between occupational National Vocational Qualifications (NVQs) introduced in 1986 and academic qualifications. They were aimed at 16–19 year olds in full-time education. Offered at three levels (Foundation, Intermediate, Advanced)
2000	Advanced Vocational Certificate in Education (AVCE)
	Replaced GNVQs at level 3. AVCEs formed part of the new Labour government's commitment to upgrade vocational qualifications and to bring GNVQs more in line with A-levels
2005	Applied A-levels
	A-levels in applied subjects. Replaced AVCE at level 3
2008	14–19 Diploma
	Offered at three levels (Foundation, Higher, Advanced). Withdrawn by the Coalition Government in 2010 and ended 2012
2014	In 2013, it was announced that all vocational qualifications were to be designated either Applied General qualifications or Tech levels from September 2014.
	Applied General qualifications (broad study of a vocational area) and Tech levels (more occupationally specific, leading to recognised occupations, for example in engineering, IT, accounting or hospitality)

were not ready for employment or occupational training. In contrast, BTECs and the succession of broad, vocational qualifications introduced alongside them since the 1990s were positioned as a middle route or bridge between academic and vocational qualifications, and since 2000, general vocational qualifications have been increasingly defined as an 'applied' version of academic qualifications, though they are supposed to provide a route into employment as well as higher-level education.

Research into these routes and qualifications suggests that conceptualisations of knowledge have been shaped by perceptions of the sorts of students who have tended to follow them and their role in the transition of these young people from education to work (Bathmaker, 2002; Bloomer & Hodkinson, 1999, 2000; Ecclestone, 2002; Hodkinson, 1998; Further Education Development Agency et al., 1997). Moreover, the links between these programmes and occupations and employment may be very tenuous; as James and his colleague found in a study of FE in the 2000s (James & Biesta, 2007), in vocationally related courses, there were often "no substantial employer links or even work experience". They observed that successful students "learned how to be good students of business studies, not how to be business employees". (James & Biesta, 2007: 77–78)

Knowledge in general vocational education: Applied, technical and vocational?

The positioning of general vocational education means that the question of 'knowledge' in these qualifications is fraught with complexity. How much emphasis should be placed on specialist theoretical knowledge, on practical knowledge and on workplace knowledge and skills and how are these connected together for students?

Michael Young (2008) proposes that knowledge in vocational education needs to provide access to the knowledge that is transforming work based on subject disciplines or broad occupational fields; it should enable students to learn job-specific skills and knowledge, which tend to be equated with 'everyday' knowledge, and teach the generic skills now required in the workplace. Young emphasises the importance of engaging with context-independent knowledge, because it "can provide a basis for generalizations and explanations that go beyond specific cases" (Young, 2008: 166), but he also states that learners need to understand the different internal structuring, contents and purposes of theoretical and everyday forms of knowledge so that they grasp the relation of the two forms to one another.

Richard Pring, who led the *Nuffield Review of 14–19 Education and Training* in England in the 2000s (Pring *et al.*, 2009) talks of applied, rather than vocational knowledge. The example of Applied Science from the *Nuffield Review* (Nuffield Review of 14–19 Education and Training, 2008) provides an illustration of how knowledge is conceptualised here. The review document explains that Applied Science involves understanding scientific knowledge and methods of scientific enquiry, which are embodied in techniques used by scientists and developed in teaching and learning through authentic work-related contexts. There is a focus on the people who apply scientific techniques and knowledge, which includes looking into the thought processes and skills involved, such as questioning the theoretical and practical limitations of a given technique that determine its application to different problems. There are opportunities for practical problem solving, emphasising the ability to use techniques, skills and knowledge for tackling science-related problems.

The aforementioned definitions of knowledge in general vocational education involve processes of what Evans and colleagues and Guile (Evans *et al.*, 2010; Guile, 2006) describe as recontextualisation, moving knowledge from disciplines and workplaces into a curriculum and from curriculum into successful pedagogic strategies. In the next section, which reports on findings from the Knowledge in Vocational Education project, the focus is particularly on pedagogic recontextualisation – that is how different forms of knowledge are organised, structured

Table 9.2 School and college research sites

Subject/Level	Site
Performing Arts Level 2	City Centre College
Performing Arts Level 3	City Centre College
Business Level 2	Rural High School
Business Level 2	City Centre College
Business Level 3	Midlands High School
Business Level 3	City Centre College
Applied Science Level 2	Outer London College
Applied Science Level 2	City Centre Sixth Form Centre
Applied Science Level 3	Outer London College

and sequenced into learning activities for the purposes of effective learning and teaching. Evans *et al.* (2010) emphasise that this process is 'tricky':

> It involves teachers, tutors, trainers making decisions about how much time they devote to and what strategies they use to explain the background to different forms of knowledge. [...] These decisions are never technical matters. They are inevitably influenced by teachers', tutors' and trainers' assumptions (often un-articulated) about what constitutes good learning experiences and worthwhile learning outcomes, and also by the specifications set by professional or examination bodies.
>
> (Evans *et al.*, 2010: 247)

As the definitions of vocational and applied knowledge outlined earlier indicate, recontextualisation in educational settings that are focused on young people influences the nature of that recontextualisation. In the two fieldwork examples that follow, different factors combine leading to particular constructions of knowledge in the two different sites.

Methods

The fieldwork for phase 2 of the Knowledge in Vocational Education Project involved qualitative case studies in nine different subject sites, located in colleges and schools in England. These sites taught vocational education qualifications in one of three subjects (science, performing arts or business) at level 2 (BTEC First) and level 3 (BTEC National) (European Qualifications Framework levels 3 and 4). Data collection included observations of teaching and assessment activities, post-observation interviews with teachers and questionnaires to students, as well as gathering course documentation.

The following analysis focuses on level 3 Applied Science at Outer London College and level 3 Performing Arts at City Centre College.

Level 3 Applied science at Outer London College

At Outer London College, students could decide to follow a BTEC route in Applied Science, or they could take A-levels in science subjects. For those following the BTEC route, the prospectus suggested a progression route into either employment or HE:

> This course [BTEC Level 3 Extended Diploma in Applied Science] is for you if you have an interest in science and would like to develop a career in Laboratory and Industrial Science. You can progress onto university or seek employment in a laboratory as a laboratory science technician.

However, according to the programme manager, BTEC was used primarily as a route into higher education, with about 90 per cent of students progressing to HE.

While staff had considerable experience of teaching on the BTEC programme, it was 'purely by chance', according to the programme manager, that three of the staff had relevant work experience as part of their employment background. Moreover, employer involvement in the programme proved challenging, because employers "don't want to be involved", and there were "practical issues about accommodating large groups of students in workplaces". Instead, there was a strong sense that the Applied Science route was an alternative to A-levels, aimed at students who were deemed less able to cope with the teaching and assessment methods in A-levels. Susan, one of the course tutors described how she saw the difference between the students studying A-levels and those taking BTEC:

> I think in maybe ability – I mean I don't like to say it . . . they do a lot of group work, they do a lot of presentations. [BTEC students] say "OK, what's the data, explain to me what the data is". Whereas with an A level they're just "oh what's the work, I need to get on with it" and that's it.

In practice, the knowledge that students were expected to engage with, and the ways in which this was recontextualised through teaching and learning, appeared to differ little from what was offered in academic A-levels. The teaching rooms included science laboratories as well as standard classrooms, but these were very much teaching spaces and not designed to replicate a workplace environment. While students were "expected to decide for themselves what to do for their practical", the instructions for writing up practical work shown in Figure 9.1 suggest a traditional educational approach to this work:

TASK – DO INVESTIGATION, RECORD RESULTS, WRITE UP
Make sure you –
Structure your report
Use clear headings
Past tense throughout
Excellent use of scientific language
Reference your data
Clear language

Figure 9.1 Instructions listed on the board for science practical task

Field notes from a teaching session show that specialist theoretical knowledge was taught but that this tended to involve the transmission of facts, conducted at a procedural level:

> The knowledge is identifying and listing factual information, and relating it (I'm not sure I would call it 'applying' or at least not in a cognitive sense) to everyday examples, very briefly and fleetingly. There's not a sense of sustained engagement with an idea or concept, but an overview of fields of terms and some specialist vocabulary. There is a smattering of cell biology/structure, e.g. the facts of cell structure in particular diseases.

In this fieldwork site, the recontextualisation of knowledge was strongly focused on progression and enabling students to succeed, but the main focus was progression to HE, rather than into the workplace. Teaching and learning practices were influenced by the perceived needs of lower achieving students, resulting in a more procedural engagement with specialist knowledge, while there was little evidence of engagement with knowledge that related to authentic work-related contexts.

Level 3 Performing arts at City Centre College

The Performing Arts programme at City Centre College was contextualised very differently from the earlier example. The college had high-quality facilities for performing arts, including a number of different rehearsal spaces and a theatre with state-of-the-art equipment that put on a regular programme of shows for the public. These facilities replicated the workplaces that students would find beyond the college in a similar way to college facilities for catering or hairdressing students. The vision of the head of department was that they were preparing students for careers in the performing arts industry:

> We're preparing people [through BTEC] for the future, for their careers, and their careers are within the entertainments industry. If they wish to be an actor or a dancer or a musician, they have to have those requisite practical skills. So high skills levels, really, very important in terms of co-ordination, balance etcetera, being able to sight-read if you want to be a session musician, taking your skill levels right up and beyond Grade 8. We're looking at world class, pushing them that way.

The head of department was an ex-professional dancer, and other staff, such as Amy, emphasised their background in the performing arts industry:

> was in the industry for a long time, as an actor and then as an agent and then a casting assistant at The Bill [popular TV programme in UK] for 4 years. And then I got a job at the Brit School in London where I taught Acting and Musical Theatre, stayed there for a year and a half. Moved here as a sessional tutor, and then I'd been here about a year and I took over the course, the running of the course.

The view about the types of knowledge involved in BTEC study reflected this emphasis on practice, as explained by Bill, one of the course tutors:

> Knowledge from a teacher's point of view, is those sort of skills and things that they need to know, the knowledge of the industry, so it's not just teaching them the facts, it's the attitude and what it's like in the industry and what's expected of them, and skills but also how to apply them. We can't just say "right, this is acting, learn that knowledge". It's "this is acting – right, this is how we do it and this is how you apply it", and I think that's what the knowledge is in relation to BTEC.

Alongside practical knowledge, tutors also talked about teaching theory, including genres of theatre, approaches of different directors and plays from different eras. One of the tutors, Julia, described how these were taught from a practice-based perspective:

> If we're teaching Stanislavski and naturalism there's a series of exercises that Stanislavski created and actually prepares, and we run practical classes in the theory of those exercises. So all the theory pretty much is done through the practice of doing, demonstrating how the theory works.

When asked about differences in the knowledge involved in BTEC and A-level, the head of department responded:

> I don't think there is. I think the difference is the amount of time devoted to developing specific knowledge and skills across the piece. Vocational students still have to be able to articulate and write about their understanding of composition, analytical skills, dance works, critical appraisal, and in order to get a distinction they have to do it at that A grade A-level equivalent standard. But the proportions of the skill range I think are different.

However, the 'vocational' students as the head of department described them, were those who had not done well at school and had not achieved the grades to progress to A-level study. Some were described as having 'car crash lives', with serious personal problems or experiences that had affected their capacity to succeed in education. So although both theoretical and practical knowledge formed an important part of the programme according to tutors, the students needed particular approaches to teaching and learning in order to succeed, as described in the following quotes:

> They are people who need direction, structure to their programmes and classes, they really do need that firmness.
> (Head of Department)

> Saying: "right, go off in your own groups and work" they can't do it, they need someone there all the time to go "right, let's do this, what are you doing?"
> (Bill, course tutor)

The students' literacy skills were seen as strong enough for the demands of advanced A-level study:

> They should be able to write about it. But taking written work . . . it's like an 11 year old has written it, it's really, really bad. And then I say to them "oh do you struggle with your writing, shall we offer you some support?" And yet they got a B at GCSE.
>
> (Anna, course tutor)

On the one hand, therefore, the recontextualisation of knowledge in the Performing Arts site was influenced by the view that this was a practice-based route. Knowledge involved specialist theoretical knowledge, but there was a strong emphasis on learning practical skills and how to apply them and learning about what the industry was like and what was expected within an authentic performing arts context, located within the college. At the same time, teaching and learning was designed to meet the needs of students who were not good at working independently, and whose literacy skills were weak. While employment in the entertainment industry was defined as the main goal, the college strongly promoted its higher-level courses in Performing Arts, and realistic progression from level 3 was more likely to be on to further education and training, than moving into employment in the industry.

Discussion and conclusions

While it is not surprising that there was a much greater link to practice and workplace settings in Performing Arts compared with Applied Science, these two examples draw attention to a number of issues that are important in any debates about knowledge in general vocational education. First, lecturers at both sites understood specialist, theoretical knowledge as an important part of the qualifications they were teaching. The challenge they faced was how to make the theoretical knowledge accessible, and as data from the Applied Science site indicates, how to move beyond the transmission of procedural knowledge to a deeper and more critical engagement with specialist knowledge in order that such knowledge could, as Young (2008) suggests, provide a basis for generalizations and explanations that go beyond specific cases. In contrast, the importance of applied and job-specific knowledge and skills appeared to depend on the background experience and orientation of lecturers, as well as access to appropriate resources and settings. The Applied Science setting demonstrates the difficulty of providing opportunities for the workplace recontextualisation of knowledge (Evans *et al.*, 2010) in the absence of a sustained and high-quality contribution from employers. In the Performing Arts, this problem was overcome by creating a workplace environment within the college, which sought to replicate experience of the industry beyond the college. Finally, at both sites, pedagogic recontextualisation of knowledge was strongly influenced by perceptions of the needs and capabilities of students taking general vocational qualifications. Lecturers at both sites described these students as lower achievers, who needed more support and guidance than their peers who were following academic A-level routes.

These issues are not new. General vocational qualifications have a long-established place in the provision of education and training for young people in England, and the raising of the participation age means that more young people are like to follow this pathway. The problematic nature of their content, their role and their purpose has been an enduring concern for researchers, which has not been resolved by the continuous succession of reforms to these qualifications. For what these reforms do not address is the ways in which practice, the pedagogic recontextualisation of knowledge on the ground, is shaped by the conditions and resources available, as well as the perceived needs of students who participate in these qualifications. A deeper consideration of how to make specialist, theoretical knowledge as well as applied and work-related knowledge accessible to students who are often middle and lower achievers, might help to address the continuing question of how to ensure that the general vocational route is not just a second chance route, but offers high-quality education to those who follow it.

Acknowledgements

This chapter is based on the work of the Knowledge in Vocational Education Project team, and my thanks go to the other members of the research team, Kathryn Ecclestone (University of Sheffield) and Sandra Cooke (University of Birmingham).

Notes

1 Level 2 in the English National Qualifications Framework = level 3 in the European Qualifications Framework. Level 3 in the English National Qualifications Framework = level 4 in the European Qualifications Framework. See http://ec.europa.eu/education/lifelong learning-policy/doc44 _en.htm.
2 Additional Tables Rates SFR 19/2015, Table A13: Participation in Education and Training of 16–18-Year-Dlds, England, 1985 Onwards. https://www.gov.uk/government/statistics/participation-in-education-training-and-employment-age-16-to-18-2
3 BTEC, part of Edexcel, is owned by Pearson. It is one of the main awarding bodies for qualifications in England.

References

Banks, M., Bates, I., Breakwell, G., Bynner, J., Elmer, N., Jamieson, I. and Roberts, K. (1992) *Careers and Identities: Adolescent Attitudes to Employment, Training and Education, Their Home Life, Leisure and Politics*. Buckingham: Open University Press.
Bates, I. (1984) *Schooling for the Dole?: The New Vocationalism*. London: Macmillan.
Bates, I. and Riseborough, G. (1993) *Youth and Inequality*. Buckingham: Open University Press.

Bathmaker, A.M. (2002) Wanting to be somebody: Post-16 students' and teachers' constructions of full-time GNVQ in a college of further education. Unpublished PhD thesis, University of Warwick.

Bathmaker, A.M. (2013) Defining 'knowledge' in vocational education qualifications in England: an analysis of key stakeholders and their constructions of knowledge, purposes and content. *Journal of Vocational Education & Training*, 65(1), 87–107.

Bloomer, M. and Hodkinson, P. (1999) *College Life: the Voice of the Learner*. London: Further Education Development Agency.

Bloomer, M. and Hodkinson, P. (2000) Learning careers: Continuity and change in young people's dispositions to learning. *British Educational Research Journal*, 26(5), 538–597.

Department for Education (DfE) (2015) Participation in education, training and employment by 16–18 year olds in England: End 2014. SFR 19 2015. https://www.gov.uk/government/statistics/participation-in-education-training-and-employment-age-16-to-18-2 (Accessed January 2016).

Ecclestone, K. (2002) *Learning Autonomy in Post-16 Education. The Politics and Practice of Formative Assessment*. London: Routledge/Falmer.

Evans, K., Guile, D., Harris, J. and Allan, H. (2010) Putting knowledge to work: A new approach. *Nurse Education Today*, 30(3), 245–251.

Further Education Development Agency, Institute of Education and The Nuffield Foundation (1997) *GNVQs 1993–1997, A National Survey Report*. London: FEDA.

Guile, D. (2006) Learning across contexts. *Educational Philosophy and Theory*, 38(3), 251–268.

Higher Education Funding Council for England (HEFCE) (2015) *Young Participation in Higher Education: A-levels and Similar Qualifications*. Bristol: HEFCE.

Hodkinson, P. (1998) Choosing GNVQ. *Journal of Education and Work*, 11(2), 151–165.

James, D. and Biesta, G. (eds.) (2007) *Improving Learning Cultures in Further Education*. London: Routledge.

The Nuffield Review of 14–19 Education and Training (2008) Issues Paper 9. Applied Learning. The Case of Applied Science, www.nuffield14–19review.org.uk (Accessed September 2010).

Pring, R., Hayward, G., Hodgson, A., Johnson, J., Keep, E, Oancea, A., Rees, G., Spours, K. and Wilde, S. (2009) *Education for All: The Future of Education and Training for 14–19 Year Olds*. London: Routledge.

Wolf, A. (2011) *Review of Vocational Education*. London: Department of Education.

Young, M. (2008) *Bringing Knowledge Back In: From Social Constructivism to Social Realism in the Sociology of Education*. London: Routledge.

10 Higher vocational learning and knowledgeable practice
The newly qualified practitioner at work

Karen Evans

Introduction

Approaches to the long-standing challenges of 'integrating' subject-based and work-based knowledge in higher vocational learning have typically focused on questions of how learning can be 'transferred' from one setting to another, relating the assumed 'abstract' nature of theory to the assumed 'real' nature of practice. This is often seen as a single movement, as encapsulated in the term 'from theory to practice'. A fresh approach that takes a more differentiated approach to forms of knowledge has examined the ways in which these forms are contextualised and 'recontextualised' in movements between different sites of learning in colleges and workplaces (Evans *et al.*, 2009).

The point of departure for this paper is that all forms of knowledge are contextual but not context bound, introducing fresh thinking about the theory-practice relation by recognising that all the forms of knowledge included in higher vocational learning (or indeed vocational learning at any level) have already been recontextualised – that is changed in the move from one context to another to serve a new purpose – and that the pedagogic challenge facing both education professionals and professionals who educate, is to support learners actively to further recontextualise forms of knowledge, using and reworking knowledge in different ways in different contexts, in relation to different purposes. In this approach, the work environment is as important as a locus for knowledge production and critical understanding as the classroom.

Higher vocational education and learning through practice

What vocational education students learn in and through the workplace or 'practice setting' entails not only the development of specific skills or competences but also a process of becoming knowledgeable through activities, roles and social practices, as well as professional identity formation. These learning processes may occur within placements which are part of the vocational programme, and they may take place after the programme, as the graduates take up positions that enable or require further workplace-based learning. All transitions to employment involve substantial new learning. In some cases, the transition is itself structured by the employer or profession, for example in law, firm-based 'training contracts' offer periods of recognised practice-based training; preceptorships in nursing are intended to structure the post-qualification stages of development; and in commercial firms, various forms of internship or graduate training schemes often fulfil this function. How transitions are experienced derives in large part from the vocational graduate's own negotiation of the fields of practice engaged in. In all cases, different forms of knowledge developed within and beyond the higher vocational programme are put to work in new and changing contexts.

This paper extends beyond existing exemplars of higher vocational programmes based on 'education-industry partnerships' (see Evans *et al.*, 2009) to consider how different forms of knowledge are developed post-qualification, as new entrants become more deeply involved in workplace practices than they are able to in placements. These ideas have themselves developed in the context of research which has yielded fresh ways of thinking about the ways in which different forms of knowledge are put to work, offering new insights into how newly qualified workers can be supported in their development as knowledgeable practitioners.

Work-based and practice-based learning in higher vocational learning

The development of higher vocational programmes has been largely driven by considerations of the organisational arrangements for work-based elements and technical issues that accompany credit and quality assurance frameworks. The knowledge dimensions have been relatively neglected. Work-based learning is defined here as learning that derives its purposes from the contexts of employment; practice-based learning similarly derives its purposes from beliefs and methods held in common by an occupational group. Thus work-based and practice-based learning have substantial areas of overlap but also differentiated features. Work-based learning, for example often emphasises the regulatory frameworks inherent in the employment relationship; practice-based learning emphasizes the regulatory frameworks and practices of the professional bodies. Higher vocational programmes that incorporate substantial elements of work-based learning bring disciplinary, work-based and practice-based knowledge together in ways that present curriculum and pedagogic challenges for lecturers and workplace mentors. Discipline-based knowledge has a different 'logic' from practice-based and work-based knowledge. The former develops through codified rules that can be used to select and combine theories and concepts into modules. In contrast, practice-based learning involves a good deal of 'procedural' knowledge, some highly codified according to rules and systems (e.g. legal) and others less codified, and work-based learning involves getting to grips with, what is sometimes referred to as, 'work process' knowledge (Boreham *et al.*, 2004). In the case of discipline-based knowledge, learners have been expected to 'apply' it to practice. In the case of work-based knowledge, learners are often assessed in accordance with competence-based criteria that are themselves heavily contested (see Hager, 2011), as programme designers struggle to articulate the relationship between discipline-based, practice-based and work-based knowledge. As Eraut's (2004) evidence has shown, participants in higher vocational learning often take a considerable time upon graduation to think and feel their ways into using their knowledge at work.

The two-year research project – Putting Knowledge to Work (PKtW)[1] responded to the challenges of finding ways of improving practice in HE programmes with substantial work-based elements (WBL) by researching how the subject-based and work-based aspects of a curriculum or learning programme can better articulate with one another. Exemplar programmes from banking, aircraft engineering, media practice, financial services, management development (glass industry) and leadership development (civil service) were analysed to identify what is involved in successfully moving knowledge from disciplines, professional fields and workplaces into a curriculum and from a curriculum into successful pedagogic strategies and learner engagement at the HE level in educational institutions and workplaces.[2] The idea of modes of knowledge recontextualisation was used heuristically, leading to the development of a novel framework of wider potential application by both researchers and practitioners. Exemplars drawn from aircraft engineering, finance, glass industry, media practice and public administration have previously been published in detail to explain the modes of recontextualisation and the developing PKtW framework. While the framework cannot itself be transferred to other occupational fields without contradicting our main underlying principle – since it too has to be recontextualised – its potential as an intellectual tool is increasingly recognized for rethinking some of the assumptions and existing practices in fields with the long-established experience of practice-based learning, e.g. nursing and medical education (see Allan *et al.*, 2010). Furthermore, vocational and professional learning continue after qualification. In the case of nursing, the period of 'preceptorship' is crucial for knowledge recontextualisation for newly qualified nurses (NQNs). In fields such a media practice, knowledge recontextualisation takes on new and often unpredictable dimensions as newly qualified graduates become 'freelancers' in a changing short-term contract market.

Explaining 'recontextualisation'

Recontextualisation refers here to the ways in which different forms of knowledge are drawn on, used and changed as they are put to work in practice settings. The development of the concept has drawn on developments of Bernstein's idea that concepts change as they move from their disciplinary origins and become a part of a curriculum (Barnett, 2006; Bernstein, 2000). Furthermore, the concept enlarged van Oers's (1998) idea that concepts are an integral part of practice and to embrace the ways in which learners themselves change as they recontextualise concepts and practices at work. Four modes of recontextualisation are significant in higher vocational learning:

CONTENT RECONTEXTUALISATION
 – putting knowledge to work in programme design*
PEDAGOGIC RECONTEXTUALISATION
 – putting knowledge to work in teaching and facilitating learning*
WORKPLACE RECONTEXTUALISATION
 – putting knowledge to work in the workplace *
LEARNER RECONTEXTUALISATION
 – what learners make of these processes

Content recontextualisation is driven by the decisions curriculum planners have to make about how to incorporate and sequence disciplinary, work process and procedural knowledge in a curriculum, while reconciling and making sense of the different knowledge logics involved. Pedagogic recontextualisation (PR) takes place as different forms of knowledge are organised, structured and sequenced into learning activities, options and modules for the purposes of effective learning and teaching. PR is also far from straightforward, as these decisions are never technical matters. They are inevitably influenced by teachers', tutors' and trainers' assumptions (often unarticulated) about what constitutes good learning experiences and worthwhile learning outcomes and also by the specifications set by professional or examination bodies. While the interplay of different knowledge forms starts with content and pedagogic recontextualisations, workplace environments play a critical role in extending the interplay it, as workplace recontextualisation, takes place through participation in the workplace practices and activities that support knowledge development and through the mentorship, coaching and other arrangements through which learners/employees can engage with and learn through workplace environments.

These practices and activities are fundamental to learners beginning to vary and modify existing workplace activities and to developing the confidence and capability to work with others to significantly change those activities. They allow us to see that we constantly and progressively recontextualise knowledge in activity. In the workplace, knowledge is embedded in routines, protocols and artefacts as well as in organisational hierarchies and power structures. New entrants learn to participate in workplace activities and to use artefacts, and they are confronted with work problems that require them to operationalise, in the contingencies of the present moment, what they know (theoretically, procedurally, interpersonally and tacitly) and have learned in a variety of teaching, practice and personal contexts. Moreover, this knowledge usually has to be used interactively in working with others. The process can be facilitated when workplaces create environments for working and learning that are both flexible and supportive and when learners are explicitly encouraged to take responsibility for observing, inquiring, collaborating and seeking help when needed.

Learner recontextualisation takes place through the strategies learners themselves use to bring together knowledge gained through the programme and gleaned from working with more experienced people in the workplace. These strategies sometimes involve learners in the creation of new knowledge, insights and activities. The learner recontextualisation process is critical to the development of a professional identity. The challenge in higher vocational degree programmes is to use knowledge as a set of resources to develop professional and academic identity together, using both curriculum and workplace knowledge in responding to the demands of practice and practice development. The process of thinking and feeling one's way into a professional identity may be facilitated by such practices as engaging in learning conversations and hearing accounts of critical incidents or difficult experiences, voicing (articulating) developing understandings of others, collaborating in teams to find solutions in less predictable situations and responding to activities that stretch capabilities beyond so-called comfort zones.

The recontextualisation framework (see Evans *et al.*, 2010; Evans & Guile, 2012), which was originally developed heuristically through research into programmes and practices in exemplar higher vocational education programmes (including engineering, finance and media practice) has been extended through new inquiries into work-based learning of 'freelancers' and the professional development of NQNs.

This paper goes beyond the original exemplars to focus on the progressive recontextualisations that take place in the workplace as newly qualified workers build on their initial vocational learning. The goal of vocational learning at this stage, I argue, is for new entrants to develop as knowledgeable practitioners, whether as employees or 'freelance' workers. The development of knowledgeable practice is a key ingredient for the involvement of workers in workplace change and development. Knowledgeable practice is practice that is characterized by the exercise of attuned and responsive judgment when individuals or teams are confronted with complex tasks and unpredictable situations at work. The concept of knowledgeable practice enables us to focus on the practice while attending to the knowledge frameworks that underpin the directing of work and the exercise of judgment that is involved in working with others to vary or change practices or products at work (Evans, 2009; Evans, 2015). How, then, is the knowledge that underpins knowledgeable practice developed? Knowledge recontextualisations extend far beyond forging connections between theory and practice. In the workplace, chains of recontextualisation are forged day by day as, for example people are stretched and challenged at work and have to exercise judgment in making decisions and taking action. Reflection on and in practice, much rehearsed in the literature, is insufficient unless it is connected to deliberation and action-taking. Chains of knowledgeable recontextualisation can be forged in different directions and from different starting points. It has already been argued that curriculum designers recast disciplinary knowledge (from its disciplinary origins) and workplace knowledge (from its professional and/or vocational contexts) and combine them in learning programmes to lay the foundations for knowledgeable practice.

Teachers choose pedagogic strategies, such as 'real-life' case studies or problem-based learning to prefigure the demands of practice for new entrants to the labour market (or to simulate new situations through 'learning labs' for experienced workers). But, most importantly, knowledgeable practice develops through learning; through the workplace itself; through observation of others; through mentorship, coaching and peer learning; and through drawing on new ideas and experiences accessed through work and, often, beyond work. These practices are fundamental to workers beginning to vary and modify existing workplace activities, or to working with experienced others to change them in the face of unexpected occurrences or the need to find new solutions. Timetabled instruction and induction sessions can introduce codified aspects of procedural and work process knowledge that are particular to the organisation, but, unlike disciplinary or subject knowledge, where there are clear criteria for structuring knowledge towards the goal of greater abstraction and depth in understanding, there are few rules about how to structure and sequence the content towards the goal of knowledgeable practice. Knowledge recontextualisation takes place when the newly qualified worker recognises a new situation as requiring a response and uses knowledge – theoretical, procedural and tacit – in acts of interpretation in an attempt to bring the activity and its setting under conscious control (van Oers, 1998).

The following analysis shows how both adaptive and productive forms of knowledge recontextualisation combine to support the development of knowledgeable practice. When the newly qualified worker analyses a work situation as requiring the enactment of a well-known activity in a new setting, an adaptive form of recontextualisation takes place, as existing knowledge is used to reproduce a response in a parallel situation. Where the interpretation of the work situation leads the newly qualified worker to change the activity or its context in an attempt to make a response, a productive form of recontextualisation takes place, as new knowledge is produced.

Example: learning in the social relations of the operating environment

An example of how knowledgeable practice develops can be drawn from aircraft maintenance engineering, where new Foundation degree programmes have been developed for aspiring maintenance engineers whose principle responsibilities will be the testing and repair of large commercial jet aircraft and their associated equipment and systems (see Evans *et al.*, 2009). College-industry partnerships have sought to meet changing knowledge and skills requirements in the industry by providing higher vocational programmes to bridge vocational and academic qualifications. The Foundation degree programme investigated showed how science-based theoretical, technical and operational knowledge is progressively recontextualised via a principle and process of 'gradual release' from a college environment to an operational aircraft hangar. Learners are brought to the point of readiness to enter the operating environment by gradually increasing the unpredictability of tasks as the time allowed for their completion is decreased, until the conditions equate to those of the live operational setting. The final weeks of the programme, in a hangar placement, were designed to support transition into the workplace for new entrants by providing a further extension of 'gradual release', i.e. from a simulated to a controlled operational environment.

The site project manager (a senior engineer) was responsible for allocating each student to an experienced licensed engineer and/or experienced fitter at supervisor grade. The project manager's expertise was particularly appreciated because it controlled the pressures on the new entrants, representing the embodiment of authority, discipline and 'duty of care'. Entry into the workplace was closely managed, with students who were close to graduation learning alongside experienced engineers subject to real-life time and commercial pressures. In the hangar, the learners extended the relation between theory and practice. They began to participate legitimately, albeit peripherally, in the rules, procedures and relationships of the organisation through 'shadowing', 'watching how others do things' and 'assisting'. In the hangar, experienced workers involved newly qualified entrants in collaborative activities, not only in jointly assessing the job but also, in the words of one supervisor, in getting

> acquainted with the daily complexities, social relations, protocols of hangar life – the pace and speed of things, the frustrations, the amount of effort that has to be put in to make the job work . . . planning it, what tools are needed and getting on with it.

As the trainee entered the operational setting, the realities and social relations of work came into play and judgment started to develop. Good supervisory support was essential in this process.

Some workplace engineers, who had followed very different pathways to qualification, considered that the Foundation degree (Fd) gradual release approach had made the learning process 'too academic' and that this made it harder for them to pass on their knowledge and skill. Some initially experienced a loss of control over the new entrants to the hangar and, as a result, felt the new entrants were 'not able to do the job'. This had an initial impact on the workplace recontextualisation process when students graduated and many became the new 'home-grown' workforce as they worked their way up through the sponsoring company:

> It took a while for people to sort out if we were any good coming out at the end – now it's not too bad – people are aware of the course and aware that the people coming out aren't completely rubbish.
>
> (Fd Graduate)

Acceptance as a member of the hangar community was important to the learners. Although these Fd graduates could work as mechanics in the industry after 2,400 hours of study, they still required structured support for learning during their two years' post-Fd experience, as they worked towards the award of their full licenses and the ability to 'sign off' on their own work. In practice, the new entrants slowly encounter more and more working time constraints, operational pressures and unpredictable circumstances; they are able to deepen their understanding of the knowledge that they have already gained and to demonstrate to their workplace supervisors that they are ready to be awarded their full licenses. As the new entrants to the workplace from this programme spent more time in the workplace, they reported their gradual recognition that "there isn't anything that hasn't been of use"; "it's all background knowledge"; "all the theory has played a part" and, moreover, they value having learnt "the background theory about why because it helps you know why a particular part is on the aircraft".

In this particular case of a tailored company-college designed programme, the learner recontextualisation process was aided by the cultural synchronicity between the college and the hangar environments. The college setting mirrored the industry in the respect that social relations and work organisation were disciplined by safety imperatives in all parts of the programme. Despite this, new entrants still experienced what some described as 'a jump'. Although it "all seems to click into place when you see it on the aircraft", and "instructors prepared us as well as they could", the experience of the jump was articulated in this way by a new worker: "it's always a bit of an in-the-deep-end kind of thing", not least because "working on a plane that you and your family could get on next week" is very different from "working on aircraft that no-one will use".

Knowledgeable practice, in this example, becomes progressively honed and widened in scope. The development of 'rounded' engineers who are knowledgeable in the core disciplines, technically proficient with an appreciation of workplace realities in getting the job done, provided a strong foundation for developmental learning at work and for the new entrant to start contributing to the development of work practices.

For graduates who did not secure a permanent position in the sponsoring company, learner recontextualisation involved navigating other hangar placements and more uncertain environments in which they had to work to convince others of the value of the programme, which was unfamiliar to many employers. Sometimes the post-qualification experience meant having to cast their net wide, to work in other countries or in internships to gain wider experience, with the prospect of proving oneself sufficiently to be taken on by the company.

Example: How do newly qualified nurses (NQNs) learn to delegate?

Nursing as a field entails the selection and organisation of subject knowledge for the demands of practice from social and psychological sciences as well as (predominantly) from medicine and pharmacology, to microbiology. In degree-level programmes leading to qualification as a registered nurse, some forms of knowledge (e.g. biomedicine) are valued more than others, depending on different tutors' preferences and different university traditions; some forms of knowledge are privileged by government policy, e.g. evidence-based practice, and the ascribing of value to knowledge is gendered (Davies, 1995). Learning outcomes are overtly agreed on by both education and practice in the pedagogic recontextualisation process, but academic and professional nurses have their own agendas regarding the final outcome for students (Maben *et al.*, 2006). From a practice perspective, a nurse ready to work as a registered nurse is what is wanted; from an education perspective, the student's learning has to be consolidated during the early years of practice (Chambers, 2007). In the practice setting, clinical areas are very busy, particularly in acute areas, and therefore the patient takes priority, not the learner. In this example, NQNs have to develop the complex competences of delegation as key ingredients of knowledgeable practice during their 'preceptorship' – a one-year programme that involves building confidence and competence at the start of their careers. New research into 'invisible learning' in the preceptorship in nurse education (Magnusson *et al.*, 2015) has elucidated how NQNs are supported, developed and assessed in the practice situation in their role of organising and supervising patient care. Approaching this question using the lens of knowledge recontextualisation has identified delegation as a particularly demanding area of practice for which NQNs are unprepared.

Delegation entails the transfer of responsibility for the performance of an activity from one individual to another, while retaining accountability for the outcome. Weydt (2010) has highlighted that delegation skills require sophisticated clinical judgments which have a strong influence on clinical and financial outcomes. The NQN is immediately responsible and held accountable for delegation to others and supervises those to whom care is delegated. According to Anthony and Vidal (2010), delegation, safety and the quality of care are inextricably linked and poor delegation is 'fertile ground for error'. The challenges experienced by NQNs in the first year of hospital-based practice are identified in current research (Allan *et al.*, 2014), as many struggle to verbalize how they learn to organize and delegate care effectively. These capabilities, crucial to role performance, are experienced as difficult by most NQNs. Delegation is a prime example of knowledgeable action-taking that involves the exercise of attuned and responsive judgment when confronted with complex tasks and often unpredictable situations. This aspect of knowledgeable practice is absolutely fundamental and is not captured by existing competence frameworks. The need to support developmental learning in this area is often overlooked in policy discourses about public service innovation that advocate greater nurse involvement in the improvement of day-to-day work practices. We have identified, in Magnusson *et al.* (2015), four types of 'invisible learning' involving knowledge recontextualisations that occur as NQNs make the transition from student to fully operational qualified nurse in the context of delegation and supervision. 'Learning through trial and error' is the first type, identified through interview and observation of NQNs in four hospital settings. The use of simulated situations as part of the post-qualifying transition might offer the opportunity to make and learn from 'safe mistakes' in the context of delegation and supervision to health care assistants. 'Learning from difficult experiences' is the second type, often occurring in emotionally stressful situations which need adequate support and reflective space if confidence is to be built up. Learning from colleagues informally, via observation, discussion and osmosis, is a third type, which can be invaluable to the NQN during transition, but critical skills and the development of judgment are needed in order to ensure that what they learn is beneficial to practice and to avoid the pitfalls of 'reverse delegation'. The fourth area of invisible learning, labelled as 'muddling through', often involves finding tolerably acceptable responses in care situations, but with an awareness that improvements and refinements could be made. All four forms of invisible learning point to the need for knowledge-aware mentorship to be consistently provided and combined with greater professional recognition of the ways in which NQNs are simultaneously adapting existing knowledge and developing new ways of thinking and acting as they learn to delegate, organise and supervise care effectively and safely in different practice situations.

Example: Freelancers learning through mimicry, synthesis and improvisation

A final example extends beyond the professions that share structured work entry driven by safety imperatives to illustrate the learning in action that takes place among 'freelance' film and TV workers, where creativity is a dominant rationale (see Bound *et al.*, 2013). Camera operators describe how they learn about the latest technology by reading the relevant manuals as well as viewing demonstrations on 'YouTube'. They develop judgment about light and aperture through 'trial and error'. Helping each other out on site provides opportunities for practice and learning about other roles (e.g. lighting, key grip, sound) as well as watching and evaluating others at work. All of these elements entail the capacity to access knowledge and ways of working from diverse channels and to recontextualise them in a variety of work settings. Experimentation and improvisation are important elements. For example a 'key grip' describes how his job entails drawing on and adapting a knowledge of physics in order to experiment with new camera angles (such as the suspension of the camera by a rope). Mimicry and synthesis also feature in accounts of learning, which emphasize observation of, for example camera operators who are known to be expert in different ways, with their own individual styles. Freelancers often learn a mix of styles by observation and practising themselves without supervision, to produce their own distinctive style or way of working. Other cases highlighted the capacity to 'think on your feet' as being an essential ingredient of becoming established as a sound technician. The subject knowledge of acoustics, for example has to be recontextualised to the problem at hand; the know-how and procedural knowledge entailed in using the equipment are recontextualised simultaneously. The account of knowledge use extends from the particular activity to the metalevel, which highlights the importance of critical abilities to 'read' situations quickly and to know how to navigate the rapidly changing and often unpredictable contexts of freelance work. For newly qualified entrants, networks often prove decisive in finding the kinds of work opportunities that allow the freelancers to build up a reputation in the field. Building a reputation entails demonstrating reliability in being able to adapt existing knowledge to a range of problems and also to do so in a way that is recognized as bringing fresh ideas into the creative process.

Learning with and from co-workers develops knowledgeable practice

In all three of the aforementioned examples, the power of learning with and from co-workers is highlighted. There are many ways in which workers can and do learn from each other in the normal performance of daily tasks. This applies irrespective of their individual levels of competency in that task, as Williams (2011) observes, yet the leveraging of the tacit knowledge that underlies this daily performance of tasks is rarely recognized or promoted. Knowledgeable practice requires abilities to recognize and solve problems, to draw on existing knowledge and to identify new knowledge that can be accessed through peers and supervisors' know-how and insights. Experts' resistance to peer mentoring can often be traced to the difficulties they experience in articulating their own knowledge and to the difficulties encountered by less experienced colleagues in asking the questions that can elicit tacit knowledge (Williams, 2011). Developing knowledge practice entails building the capacities to articulate and to share both tacit and explicit forms of knowledge with co-workers as a potentially effective way to improve the overall knowledge and performance of teams, departments and, ultimately, the organization.

Yet mentoring and learning with and from co-workers depend crucially on constructive interplay in the ways that management's and workers' roles are performed, which is in turn heavily influenced by the regulatory frameworks that govern the employment relationships and the quality of work environments.

Conclusions

The long-standing language of 'transfer' hinders rather than facilitates the search for solutions to the theory-practice gap. The concept of recontextualisation helps to:

- identify the ways in which all forms of knowledge are tied to context (settings where things are done)
- identify actions that assist people to move knowledge from context to context
- identify how knowledge changes as it is used differently in different social practices (ways of doing things) and contexts
- identify how new knowledge changes people, social practices and contexts
- identify who and what supports processes of recontextualisation

The lens of recontextualisation thus takes the debate beyond the 'joining' of different knowledge forms (Billett, 2009) to focus attention on underlying social processes involved in successfully moving knowledge from disciplines and workplaces into a curriculum, from a curriculum into successful pedagogic strategies and from learner/employee engagement in educational institutions and workplaces to the exercise of judgment in knowledgeable practice.

Knowledge recontextualisations are fundamental to workers beginning to enact existing workplace activities, or working with experienced others to modify and change them in the face of unexpected occurrences or the need to find new solutions. Forms of knowledge are inherent in routines, protocols and artefacts as well as in organisational hierarchies and power structures. In addition to learning to participate in workplace activities and to use protocols and artefacts, newly qualified practitioners use work problems as a further 'test bench' for theoretical and subject-based knowledge. This is facilitated when workplaces create flexible but supportive environments for working and learning and learners take responsibility for observing, inquiring and acting.

Newly qualified workers quickly learn that most work situations rely on interdependencies between co-workers, with fine balances having to be achieved between consulting colleagues and burdening them with matters in which even a beginner is expected to be competent. Losing this balance can mean either being defensive about practice or taking actions that are beyond one's competence in order to avoid 'losing face'. When newly qualified workers are also expected to manage and lead the work of teams, these challenges intensify. Self-knowledge and knowing one's own limitations are integral to the development of the attuned judgment that characterises knowledgeable practice; such self-knowledge is also developed iteratively through multiple recontextualisations, as newly qualified workers are typically deployed to work with many different colleagues and teams in the early years of practice.

Newly qualified workers, through many knowledge recontextualisations, come to self-embody knowledge cognitively and practically. Furthermore both adaptive and productive forms of knowledge recontextualisation combine to support the development of knowledgeable practice. When the newly qualified worker analyses a work situation as requiring the enactment of a well-known activity in a new setting, an adaptive form of recontextualisation takes place as existing knowledge is used to reproduce a response in a parallel situation. Where the interpretation of the work situation leads the newly qualified worker to change the activity or its context in an attempt to make a response, a productive form of recontextualisation takes place, as new knowledge is produced. In both forms of adaptive and productive recontextualisation, the higher vocational learning of a newly qualified worker has to acknowledge combinations of relationships with co-workers (including managers) in teams working together within in the wider organizational environment, while simultaneously achieving task oriented duties.

Notes

1 The project was sponsored by the London Chamber of Commerce and Industry Commercial Education Trust and the UK Economic and Social Research Council (ESRC).
2 Over the 30 months of the original research, interviews were conducted in colleges and workplaces, with learner employees during and after their programmes, with programme designers, course tutors, supervisors and workplace trainers. In the six programmes selected for in-depth research, observations were carried out during more than 53 days of site visits. The authenticity of the findings has been cross-checked with practitioners, both in the field and through advisory groups.

References

Allan, H., Magnusson, C., Horton, K., Evans, K., Ball, E., Curtis, K. and Johnson, M. (2014) People, liminal spaces and experience: Understanding recontextualisation of knowledge for newly qualified nurses. *Nurse Education Today*, 35(2), 78–83.

Anthony, M. and Vidal, K. (2010) Mindful communication: A novel approach to improving delegation and increasing patient safety. *OJIN: The Online Journal of Issues in Nursing*, 15(2), Manuscript 2. http://www.nursingworld.org/Main MenuCategories/ANAMarketplace/ANAPeriodicals/OJIN/TableofContents/Vol152010/No2May2010/Mindful-Communication-and-Delegation.html. (Accessed 21 December 2015).

Barnett, M. (2006) Vocational knowledge and vocational pedagogy, in M. Young and J. Gamble (eds.) *Knowledge, Curriculum and Qualifications for South African Further Education*. Cape Town: HSRC Press, pp. 143–158.

Bernstein, B. (2000) *Pedagogy, Symbolic Control and Identity: Theory, Research Critique* (Revised Edition). Lanham: Rowman and Littlefield Publishers, Inc.

Billett, S. (2009) Realising the educational worth of integrating work experiences in higher education. *Studies in Higher Education*, 34(7), 827–843.

Boreham, N., Fischer, M. and Samurçay, R. (2004) *Work Process Knowledge*. Abingdon: Routledge.

Bound, H., Rushbrook, P., Waite, E., Evans, K., Lin, M., Karmel, A., Nur, S., Sivalingam, M. and Seng, A. (2013) The entrepreneurial self: Becoming a freelancer in Singapore's film and television industry. http://www.voced.edu.au/content/ngv62193 (Accessed 5 May 2015).

Chambers, D. (2007) Is the modern NHS fit for nursing students? *British Journal of Nursing*, 16(2), 74–75.

Davies, C. (1995) *Gender and the Professional Predicament of Nursing*. Buckingham: Open University Press.

Eraut, M. (2004) *Developing Professional Knowledge: A Review of Progress and Practice*. London: Falmer Press.

Evans, K. (2009) *Learning, Work and Social Responsibility*. Dordrecht: Springer.

Evans, K. (2015) Developing knowledge practice at work, in M. Elg, Per-Erik Ellstrom, M. Klofsten and M. Tillmar (eds.) *Sustainable Change and Development in Organizations*. Edward Elgar.

Evans, K. and Guile, D. (2012) Putting different forms of knowledge to work in practice, in J. Higgs, R. Barnett, S. Billett, M. Hutchings and F. Trede (eds.) *Practice-Based Education: Perspectives and Strategies*. Rotterdam, Netherlands: Sense Publishers, pp. 113–130.

Evans, K., Guile, D. and Harris, J. (2009) *Putting Knowledge to Work*. London: Institute of Education. http://eprints.ioe.ac.uk/17916/1/Research_briefing_60.pdf (Accessed 5 May 2015)

Evans, K., Guile, D. and Harris, J. (2009) Putting knowledge to work: The exemplars. http://eprints.ioe.ac.uk/17916/2/book_of_exemplars.pdf (Accessed 5 May 2015)

Evans, K., Guile, D., Harris, J. and Allan, H. (2010) Putting knowledge to work: A new approach. *Nurse Education Today*, 30(3), 245–251.

Hager, P. (2011) Theories of workplace learning, in M. Mallcoh, L. Cairns, K. Evans and B. O'Connor (eds.) *The Sage Handbook of Workplace Learning*. London: Sage, pp. 17–31.

Maben, J., Latter, S. and Macleod Clark, J. (2006) The theory-practice gap: Impact of professional-bureaucratic work on newly qualified nurses. *Journal of Advanced Nursing*, 55(4), 465–477.

Magnusson, C., Westwood, S., Ball, S., Curtis, K., Evans, K., Horton, K., Johnson, M., and Allan, H. (2015) An investigation into newly qualified nurses' ability to recontextualise knowledge to allow them to delegate and supervise care (AaRK). http://surreyweblb.surrey.ac.uk/fhms/research/centres/crnme/currentactivity/AaRK%20project/aark-summary-report.pdf (Accessed 5 May 2015)

van Oers, B. (1998) The fallacy of decontextualisation. *Mind, Culture and Activity*, 5(2), 143–52.

Weydt, A. (2010) Developing delegation skills. *The Online Journal of Issues in Nursing*, 15(2), manuscript 1.

Williams, D. (2011) An investigation into tacit knowledge management at the supervisory level. PhD thesis. University of Waikato. http://researchcommons.waikato.ac.nz/handle/10289/5743 (Accessed 5 May 2015)

11 Conclusion
Global perspectives on vocationalism and the English model

Jill Jameson and Sai Loo

From a global perspective, vocational education and training (VET) may be seen in general in wider international contexts as a possible educational approach for young people of pre-university age who perhaps lack the educational abilities, motivation, confidence, funding and social capital (or any combination of these) to undertake academic study either immediately or in the longer term. It may also be seen as a possible route into employment in order to improve students' life chances (Quintini & Martin, 2006). Furthermore, vocational provision may involve older students as well as young adults and existing employees on work-based training schemes. VET provision is also frequently linked to specific national educational policies that aim to improve economic competitiveness, workforce development, skills, entrepreneurship and employability. In some countries, policies for vocational education are also linked to government aims to increase social mobility and social justice, to diversify and equalise workforce achievement and to address specific needs of poorer and marginalised population groups. The manifestations of such aims are embedded within different cultures and societies in varied ways across the world. In many systems, though not all, VET functions as a 'second-chance' route of lesser status than academic provision. In many systems, though again, not all, issues of gender, ethnic minority, economic and social class inequalities may underpin VET systems linked to various occupations, while patterns of social and cultural divisions may complicate employment outcomes. VET systems may (or may not) also be aligned to higher education systems, community partnerships and employer training schemes. VET systems are also in various ways linked with national vocational qualifications frameworks and inspection systems.

Eichlorst *et al.* (2014) offer a typology of international VET systems based on national supply-side provision – namely, 1) vocational and technical schools, 2) vocational training centres, 3) formal apprenticeships, 4) dual apprenticeship systems that combine school training with a 'firm-based' approach and 5) informal-based training. While such typologies can be limitingly superficial and may not sufficiently recognise the multiple evolutions – distinctive cultures and social traditions that affect vocational learning in local national contexts – this basic characterisation at the level of the supply of systems of provision is useful. At one end of this notional international VET systems spectrum – from formal vocational schools through apprenticeships models to informal learning – some vocational schools do not offer work-based training, while, at the other end, some apprenticeships and informal learning approaches exclude formal theoretical curricular input. There is, also, within that very broad notion of a global VET continuum, enormous international diversity, much overlapping or idiosyncratic local provision that does not quite 'fit' anywhere and a relentlessly ever-changing series of complexities in the interpretation of 'vocationalism'. In summing up this book in the context of the 'English model' of vocationalism, it is important, therefore, to recognise the tentative provisionality of any kind of sweeping global categorisation, given the huge diversity and complexity of scope involved. It is also important to critique the fallibility of any attempt at 'one size fits all' global typologies. Nevertheless, at the 'helicopter' level of understanding, we can locate some key areas in which the way of organising and delivering vocational education and training within England tends to align with and/or differ from that in other countries. This broad-brush summary analysis suggests ways in which the English model may be placed alongside those of other countries in order that we might begin to learn how to improve the effectiveness of the policies, practices, funding, employer involvement and student take-up of the VET provision in England.

This is a challenging task, given Coffield's (2006) analysis of the varied dysfunctionalities of the English educational landscape, in which we may observe that vocational education and training sits rather imperfectly within and also overlaps a broader notion of 'post-compulsory education', which itself is rather uncomfortably positioned as the miscreant poorer 'middle child' (Foster, 2005) of the educational 'system' in England:

> England does not have an educational system, but instead three badly co-ordinated sectors – Schools, Post Compulsory Education and HE – which reflect sharp divisions within the Department of Education and Skills (DfES). The mental image suggested by these structural arrangements is of three well-intentioned but dyspraxic and myopic elephants, who are constantly bumping into each other and standing on each other's feet instead of interweaving smoothly in one elegant dance.
>
> (Coffield, 2006)

To expand this analysis of the ways in which English vocational education differs from others into an international comparison, there is a need to understand the ways in which it has been shaped (or mis-shaped) by successive government-led initiatives during past decades. Ewart Keep (2006) has described the strongly interventionist English central government state-led engagement with education and training using the phrase: 'playing with the biggest train set in the world'. Keep observes that, paradoxically, despite continuous rhetorical insistence on the need for a reduction of the state, the importance of the market and the need for meso and micro levels of 'demand-led' ownership, in England, the voluntarist nature of employer engagement has underpinned a continuing failure to let others outside of government play with the education and training train set (Keep, 2006).

Furthermore, in an interesting article comparing the English educational instructional system for 15-year-olds with those of ten high-performing countries as measured by the OECD (Organisation for Economic Co-operation and Development) Programme for International Assessment results, Creese and Isaacs (2016) observe:

> England is out of step with many of the high-performing jurisdictions, largely deliberately and at the behest of recent and current governments. It is at the deep end of centralisation, its curriculum is not much integrated, and its accountability system is high-stakes test and examinations based coupled by an exacting inspection system.
>
> (Creese & Isaacs, 2016: 151)

Within Eichlorst *et al.'s* (2014) typology of international VET systems, therefore, we may classify the English model as situated broadly within the third system identified, but also including elements of the first and second systems, as a model that delivers apprenticeships alongside vocational college, some vocational school and private vocational training provision. To analyse these systems, it is useful to consider how they are aligned, albeit imperfectly, with VET provision in various countries.

In the first model identified by Eichlorst *et al.* (2014), VET provision is offered in vocational and technical schools. This kind of VET system is offered in Southern European countries such France, Spain and Italy, along with some Middle Eastern and North African countries, Eastern European countries and Central African nations. This 'vocational school' approach offers young people practice-oriented knowledge and skills for specific occupations, which is combined with a formal curriculum with general and occupation-specific know-how. The second kind of approach is a variant of this: to offer VET training in specialist centres which are to differing degrees controlled and regulated by the state. For example vocational training in Latin America (e.g. Argentina, Peru and Venezuela) occurs in vocational training centres instead of schools and is aimed mainly at disadvantaged youths. The curriculum is demand-led, and is, in its later evolution, not specified by governments and combines an internship with classroom training.

By contrast, third, Eichlorst *et al.* (2014) discuss the formal apprenticeship model within their typology. To critique the typology itself, it should be noted that this kind of model tends not to be based on apprenticeships only, but on a more or less complex, country-specific mixed combination of vocational college, school-based and training provider courses with formal apprenticeships. This kind of mixed vocational route combined with apprenticeship provision is offered by countries such as the UK, including England, as well as in the US, Australia and South Africa. Formal apprenticeships tend to include both institutional input and workplace training. Vocational provision in this kind of mixed model is more or less controlled and regulated by the state, with variable employer participation. Therefore, arguably, we could propose that Eichlorst *et al.'s* third system of formal apprenticeships might combine also some elements of their first and second systems.

Fourth, the most sophisticated model, the dual vocational education and training system, which is usually regarded as the best performing of the VET systems, is widespread in Austria, Denmark, Germany and Switzerland. In this 'dual' system, there is a high degree of formalization involving social and business partners, accompanied by general and occupation-specific education that is delivered by vocational colleges or schools frequently linked to universities and supported by training firms with accredited technical standards. However, this 'dual' system tends to exclude young people who are low achievers (Solga *et al.*, 2014). Fifth, in Eichlorst *et al.*'s final model, informal-based training occurs in India and in African countries where family or clan members transmit practice-based vocational knowledge between generations in traditional apprenticeships (ILO, 2011) which may lack formal theoretical input.

Eichlorst *et al.* (2014) also offer empirical evidence on the effectiveness of each of these VET systems in turn as regards learner outcomes such as employability. First, they acknowledge that youths from school-based VET appear to perform just as well as if they had remained in academic provision and that vocational training centres provide an easier transition to gainful employment for learners with low abilities. Those graduating from apprenticeships appear to improve their employment and wage prospects by engaging in apprenticeship training, but are still behind college/university graduates, whereas those coming out of the dual systems are better at obtaining employment than those from academic education in 'dual systems' countries. However, there appeared to be no ascertainable wage differential in the latter case. Finally, those coming from informal training routes improve their employment prospects, perhaps because of their close links with connected persons and businesses (Eichlorst *et al.*, 2014). The aforementioned descriptions of the effectiveness of these five kinds of international VET systems appear in general to enhance young learners' employment prospects after they complete their training, with the dual system being the most effective vocational provision in comparison to the academic route as regards learner outcomes and employment. Needless to say, however, there is a level of complexity, infinitely variable changeability and non-transferability in any form of international comparison, and VET systems are no different from other educational provision in this regard. Furthermore, closer investigations of any VET system will throw up strengths and weaknesses: this book attempts to delineate some of these issues in relation to the 'English' model.

In this book, therefore, we consider vocationalism in relation to the post-compulsory education sector in England: 'the English model' of vocationalism, as reflected through the perceptions of a selection of academic experts gathered together here from the field. The 'English model' as described by numerous researchers (Brockmann *et al.*, 2008; Clarke & Winch, 2015; Grubb, 2004) tends to focus on specific practical individual learning outcomes for employability rather than on the wider achievement of knowledge-based occupational and citizenship development alongside and in the context of work-related skills. The English system therefore concentrates more narrowly on skills acquisition than on a combination of theoretical knowledge and workplace holistic occupational preparation.

Conclusion 135

The English vocational education system can be contrasted with 'dual' vocational systems which combine both knowledge-based learning and apprenticeships involving workplace learning in countries such as Germany, Switzerland and Austria, as Brockmann *et al.* (2008) observe in their comparative analysis of vocational education and training systems in selected countries in Europe. They conclude that "a major distinction needs to be made between two VET models: a knowledge-based model operating in Germany and the Netherlands, and a skills-based model in England" (Brockmann *et al.* (2008): 549).

The skills-based English model of VET has come in for a fair amount of criticism from policy makers, practitioners and researchers, as the contributing authors in this book either outline directly or tend to imply. Indeed, in this context, there is a somewhat bizarre irony in the fact that England (included within the UK, more broadly speaking) has been recognised for centuries for the excellence of its higher education system and contributions to professional expertise, particularly but not exclusively insofar as these are linked to the prestige of elite research-intensive universities (Blackmore, 2016; Elsevier, 2013; Hemsley-Brown, 2012). Although not generally described using the term 'vocational', higher education in England and the UK generally is also renowned for its international contributions to academic research, research impact, innovation and professional expertise in medicine, mathematics, the natural sciences, the social sciences, in literature, media studies, philosophy, politics, computing, architecture, film, physical education and music, amongst many fields of occupational endeavour (Elsevier, 2013). International comparative analyses of research performance indicate that

> While the UK represents just 0.9% of global population, 3.2% of R&D expenditure, and 4.1% of researchers, it accounts for 9.5% of downloads, 11.6% of citations and 15.9% of the world's most highly-cited articles. Amongst its comparator countries, the UK has overtaken the US to rank 1st by field-weighted citation impact (an indicator of research quality). Moreover, with just 2.4% of global patent applications, the UK's share of citations from patents (both applications and granted) to journal articles is 10.9%. The UK is a highly productive research nation in terms of articles and citation outputs per researcher or per unit of R&D expenditure.
>
> (Elsevier, 2013: 2)

Yet, simultaneously, for decades, rightly or wrongly, England, an extremely high academic, professional and research performer within the UK nations, has also been regarded, somewhat strangely, as massively underperforming in 'vocational' education. There is a deep oddity of disconnection about this, because almost every one of the accomplishments and outputs in the fields of achievement listed in the earlier paragraphs is in fact linked in some way with a 'vocation', in the sense of a professional pathway of higher employment and one or more fields of occupational knowledge. Yet these advanced level occupational fields in higher education and the professions are not considered to be part of – and not even directly connected with – the formal English 'vocational education and training system', the term 'vocational education and training' or 'VET' being reserved almost exclusively for lower-level FE and training in skills for particular jobs.

Residing within this 'English model' there is, therefore, a relatively underacknowledged but nevertheless significant social class and socio-economic status schism between (1) the achievement of higher levels of theoretical knowledge, academic and industrial research credentials and occupational status on the one hand, in HE and the professions and (2) on the other, the gaining of lower-level employability for particular jobs through the acquisition of specific skills and training in workplace learning in FE.

Criticisms of the 'English model' of vocational education and training have, as a result, tended to be centred around educational and training provision at the lower levels of what it means to be 'vocational'. This narrowness of low-skills-based vocational provision and its disconnection with higher professional achievement has possibly developed from a somewhat reductive Anglo-Saxon notion of 'learning outcomes' in vocational education (Clarke & Winch, 2015), as exemplified in competence-based National Vocational Qualifications (NVQs) that are focused more on individual outputs of the vocational system (Hyland, 1994) rather than on higher-level occupational mobility and rigour at the curricular and employer input level, as in, say, the German system. The 'English model' of VET has continued to centre increasingly on a limited, utilitarian notion of skilled employability, rather than on the learning of wider occupationally related knowledge, as Brockmann *et al.* suggest:

> [In England] . . . there has been a trend towards a narrowing down of 'skills' and a further weakening of the knowledge base. Here, a strongly demand-led system ensures the production of narrow sets of 'skills' and minimal underpinning knowledge suited to a predominantly low-skilled labour market. This raises the question whether the notion of employability as understood and put into operation in England works to the detriment of individuals by trapping them in low-skill sectors of the economy. Thus, the nature of employability reflects the differences in the conceptualisation of VET: a knowledge-based approach in Germany and the Netherlands and a skills-based approach in England.
>
> (Brockmann *et al.*, 2008: 550)

The term 'skill' in England in effect suggests the training of a lower-level worker to do a specific task in a closely behaviourist, performative and reductive way: it has a technicist underpinning that tends to belie the inclusion of broader abilities, deeper expertise, cultural context and intelligence. It, therefore, carries with it an implicit assumption of limited ability and lower achievement. The English separation between the sectors of skills-based 'vocational' and knowledge-based 'higher' education has therefore partly led to and partly arisen from divisive societal and political perceptions of vocational education and training in which there is a lack of parity of esteem between 'vocational' and 'higher' education. This has reduced the impact of vocational education provision – and its prospective connection with HE and professionalism – limiting its potential to achieve wide-ranging learning for life, to develop broader conceptions of citizenship and cultural capital, to contribute more expansively to society and to stimulate original innovations for the growth of the economy. As Ainley and Allen observe in Chapter 2, the continuing social divisions between narrowly prescribed training provision for traditional manual trades offered by FE institutions and more expansive, higher-level provision for non-manual professions provided by HE institutions has bedevilled the vocational route in England. As a result, these authors note with concern that "conditions of general downward social mobility in the new century" (Roberts, 2010) have increased as a semi-permanent 'reserve army of labour' comprising low-level 'vocational' workers at the depressed end of the 'skills' range have been recycled hopelessly between temporary, part-time or insecure low-paying jobs and periods of unemployment (see Ainley & Allen, Chapter 1). The degree of stratification and division between higher and lower achievers at each end of the spectrum of education has continued to increase as social mobility has declined and the separation between the sectors has continued.

This almost complete disconnection between HE and FE as regards policy, funding, local leadership and management, pedagogic quality and delivery of provision in England regarding 'vocationalism' is difficult to understand from a logical perspective. As Alison Wolf has observed, linking this situation to a variant of human capital theory in policy making that is based on the myth (Wolf, 2002) equating the development of 'skills' with improvements in productivity and economic growth, these divisions between higher and further education do not make sense:

> In England, regrettably, the 19+ education system is rarely discussed as an entity, or an interlocking system, even in the context of labour market demands for skills. Debates over higher education (HE) take place as though further education (FE) and adult training did not exist. . . . . . (Wolf, 2015: 2) it makes more sense than ever to think about post-19 education and training, and about government support for it, in a unified way. Instead, the system . . . which we currently operate, is more bifurcated than ever before, with a huge proportion of spending concentrated on academic three year programmes for young people, and with spending per learner far lower in the 'skills' sector than in HE.
>
> (Wolf, 2015: 66)

These ancient divisions between higher and further education need to be revisited to form new pathways to the future for an improved understanding and a new exploration of what 'vocational' education really means. The experts who have contributed to this book on vocationalism in education have reported theoretical and evidence-based empirical research findings which underpin such an exploration. Our authors have debated the educational policies, pedagogic methods, curricular content, classroom learning, teaching practices and work contexts in which 'vocationalism' takes shape. They have discussed their research findings at the levels of first, macro analysis at the national and policy-making level, second, meso analysis at the level of programmes and organisations and, finally, micro analysis in the context of individuals as learners and teachers within the vocational education system.

These three analytical focal levels, represented within the tripartite structure of the book and enriched by the contributions of differing authors, interact with each other as alternating complementary perspectives in a long debate about vocationalism. This is situated within a current context of trends towards ever-more intense globalisation, marketisation, massification and league table stratification as these affect nations, higher and further education systems, institutions and individuals across the world. Within this overall picture, the 'English model' stands out clearly in contrast to the vocational systems of other countries.

Avis's critique of the English model in Chapter 8 identifies the deficits within an Anglo-Saxon construction of vocational pedagogy that is only focused on the world of work, unlike the richer pedagogic understandings of vocationalism in other societies which offer wider forms of learning, including civic and academic education. Nevertheless, Avis proposes that, despite this, transformative and creative workforce potentials can still emerge in a post-Fordist economy.

In Avis's conception of a more promising future for 'vocationalism', workers contribute to the success of their organisations by shaping a collective intelligence that offers opportunities in egalitarian and democratic relations between workers and businesses. Could an emergent 'HIVE' concept of 'higher vocational education', in which a collective intelligence is envisaged for advanced levels of transformational learning in networked communities in a so-called knowledge society, as discussed in the ESRC HIVE-PED Research Seminar Series project linked to the contribution by Jameson, Joslin and Smith in Chapter 4, contribute to a potential understanding of new pathways in vocationalism for the future? The notion of a 'hive mind', as envisaged by Jones (2011) and others, brings with it a new potential for vocationalism in a digital age, linked to occupations and professionalism right across the higher and further education divides. This creates the potential for a comprehensive spectrum of 'occupation-related' courses/levels, from beginner through to intermediate, senior, advanced and expert levels across all of the professions and trades. Such a vision is a future reification of Alison Wolf's proposal in 2015 that, as a result of serious financial, socio-economic, qualifications and employment-related imbalances in the current highly divisive and dysfunctional vocational education system in England,

> we therefore need, as a matter of urgency, to start thinking about post-19 funding and provision in a far more integrated way.
>
> (Wolf, 2015: 76)

Such a potential for an integrated vocational/occupational/professional educational system calls for research investigations into new further and higher pathways across the currently divided higher and further sectors for the advancement of scientific, industrial, creative and innovatory business professions in the knowledge economy, completely reconceptualising and transforming the 'English model' for a new future. Specifically, we identify that English VET provision has tended to be overly dominated by central state intervention in the past few decades, that it tends to be less effective as regards learner and employment outcomes than provision in 'dual system' countries and it has tended to be driven by supplier-side economic policies rather than demand-led learner interests. It has been measured more by economic interests and targets rather than through individually focused learner goals. It has also tended to be voluntaristic as regards employer accountability and has insufficiently involved community and social partners in VET policy formation and delivery. Those involved in the English model, we argue, can learn much from international comparison.

References

Blackmore, P. (2016) *Prestige in Academic Life: Excellence and Exclusion*. Abingdon, Oxon: Routledge.

Brockmann, M., Clarke, L. and Winch, C. (2008) Knowledge, skills, competence: European divergences in vocational education and training (VET) – the English, German and Dutch cases. *Oxford Review of Education*, 34(5), 547–567.

Clarke, L. and Winch, C. (2015) Have Anglo-Saxon concepts really influenced the development of European qualifications policy? *Research in Comparative and International Education*, 10, 593–606.

Coffield, F. (2006) *Running Ever Faster Down the Wrong Road: An Alternative Future for Education and Skills*. Inaugural Lecture at the Institute of Education, 5 December, 2006. London, England: Institute of Education, University of London.

Creese, B. and Isaacs, T. (2016) International instructional systems: How England measures up. *The Curriculum Journal*, 27(1), 151–165.

Eichlorst, W., Rodriquez-Planas, N. and Zimmermann, K.F. (2014) *A Roadmap to Vocational Education and Training Around the World*. Bonn: Literaturverz. http://www.iza.org/conference_files/worldb2014/1551.pdf (Accessed 12 August 2014)

Elsevier (2013) International Comparative Performance of the UK Research Base – 2013, Report commissioned by the UK Department for Business, Innovation and Skills (BIS), London: BIS. https://www.gov.uk/government/uploads/system/uploads/attachment_data/file/263729/bis-13-1297-international-comparative-performance-of-the-UK-research-base-2013.pdf (Accessed February 2016)

Foster, A (2005) *Realising the Potential: A Review of the Future Role of Further Education Colleges*. (The Foster Report). London: DfES (Department for Education and Skills).

Grubb, W.N. (2004) The Anglo-American approach to vocationalism: The economic roles of education in England. SKOPE Research Paper 52: Universities of Oxford and Warwick. http://www.skope.ox.ac.uk/wordpress/wp-content/uploads/2014/04/SKOPEWP52.pdf (Accessed February 2016)

Hemsley-Brown, J. (2012) 'The best education in the world': Reality, repetition or cliché? International students' reasons for choosing an English university. *Studies in Higher Education*, 37(8), 1005–1022.

Hyland, T. (1994) *Competence, Education and NVQs*. London: Cassell.

International Labour Organisation (ILO). (2011) *Upgrading Informal Apprenticeships Systems. ILO Policy Brief*. Geneva: ILO.

Jones, G. (2011) National IQ and national productivity: The hive mind across Asia. *Asian Development Review*, 28(1), 51–71.

Keep, E. (2006) State control of the English education and training system – playing with the biggest train set in the world. *Journal of Vocational Education & Training*, 58(1), 47–64

Quintini, G., and Martin, S. (2006) Starting well or losing their way? The position of youth in the labour market in OECD countries. OECD Social, Employment and Migration Working Papers 39. Paris: OECD.

Roberts, K. (2010) The end of the long baby-boomer generation? If so, what next? Liverpool University Department of Sociology unpublished paper. https://guyshrubsole.files.wordpress.com/2010/12/the-end-of-the-long-baby-boomer-generation.pdf (Accessed February 2016)

Solga, H., Protsch, P., Ebner, C. and Brzinsky-Fay, C. (2014) *The German Vocational Education and Training System: Its Institutional Configuration, Strengths, and Challenges*. Berlin: WZB Berlin Social Science Centre.

Wolf, A. (2002) *Does Education Matter? Myths about Education and Economic Growth*. London: Penguin Books.

Wolf, A. (2015) Issues and ideas. Heading for the precipice: Can further and higher education funding policies be sustained? The Policy Institute at King's College London, June 2015 Report. https://www.kcl.ac.uk/sspp/policy-institute/publications/Issuesandideas-alison-wolf-digital.pdf (Accessed February 2016)

Index

16–19 Study Programmes 55

academic 108, 135
advance level (A-level) 43
advanced level apprenticeships *see* apprenticeships
Advanced Vocational Certificate of Education (AVCE) 53
agency 42
age profile 46
Ainley, P. 9, 11, 5, 18
aircraft maintenance engineering 122
Allen, M. 9, 12, 18
analogies 86
Anglo-Saxon 136
applied 109 *see* knowledge
Applied General qualifications 57, 65
apprentices/apprenticeships 9, 38, 45, 73, 74; advanced level 18; formal apprenticeship model 133; FE-HE apprenticeship qualifications 3; frameworks 11; higher-level 2, 18; intermediate 18; Modern Apprenticeships 9; pathways 41; trainees 73; wages 12
art discipline 86
Australian vocational education and training system; *see* vocationalism
Avis, J. 9, 93, 98

Bailey, B. 18
Bailey, M. 17
Barnett, M. 79
Bathmaker, A-M. 106
behaviourist 136
Bernstein, B. 79
biographical experiences 85
Blair, T. 16
boundaries 23

Bourdieu, P. 16
Brockman, M. 12
Brown, G. 16
Brynjolfsson, E. 10
budget cuts 72
bureaucracy 38, 41
Business and Technology Education Council (BTEC) 42, 107, 108, 110, 111, 113

Cable, V. 14
capitalism 93
career paths 71
centralisation 133
central state intervention 139
Certificate of Pre-Vocational Education (CPVE) 53
'chaotic landscape' 38
citizenship 93
Clandinin, J. 80
Clarke, T. 10
clinical skills 84
co-configuration 94
co-opetition 94
co-workers 127
cognitive capitalism 99
collaboration 31, 33, 34, 78, 83
collective intelligence 96
college 22–35, 124
college-industry partnerships 122
Commission on Adult Vocational Teaching and Learning (CAVTL) 100
community 25, 27, 29–30, 33–4
community of practice 60
competence frameworks 125
complexity 40, 48, 134
Confederation of British Industry (CBI) 10
connectivity 96

Index

content recontextualisation *see* recontextualisation
control 22, 26–7, 32
creative 126
cultural capital 137
curriculum 72, 79; curriculum solution 88
'curriculum-related' 79

delegation 125
democratic participation 93
dental practice 84
Department for Business, Innovation and Skills (DBIS) 12, 14, 15
designing 3
Digital Taylorism 98
diplomas 53
disadvantaged neighbourhoods 43
disciplinary knowledge 81, 86, 101
disciplines 81
disconnection 137
divisions 137
domain-wide knowledge 83
Dorling, D. 15
dual vocational education and training system *see* vocationalism
dysfunctionalities 132

economic 131
ecosystem 47
ESRC Higher Vocational Education and Pedagogy (HIVE-PED) 2, 38, 138
Education Act 2011 12
education of teachers 4
Elliott, G. 22
employability 134
employer accountability 139
Employment Act 1944 10
English context 1
'English model' 6, 132, 134, 136
English VET provision *see* vocationalism
essential knowledge 83
European Union 93
Evans K. 79, 117
everyday knowledge 86
evidence-based research 1, 78, 83
ethnic minority 131
'expansive-restrictive' 47

fees (undergraduate) 15
FE-HE 38
FE-HE apprenticeship qualifications; *see* apprenticeships
finance 27, 28, 29
financial incentives 72
Finegold, D. 19
Flexibilisation 98
flexible part-time HE 46
flexible production systems 95
Fordism 95
formal apprenticeship model; *see* apprenticeships
Foundation degrees 19, 45
frameworks *see* apprenticeships
freelancers 126
Freedman, D. 17
functional skills 11
funding 23, 26, 27, 28, 31, 33, 34, 68, 69
Furlong, A. 18
further education (FE) 11, 17, 22, 37, 38, 78

Gamble, A. 10
gender (apprentices and students) 2, 46, 69, 131
general intellect 10
generic knowledge 83
General National Vocational Qualification (GNVQ) *see* vocationalism
general vocational education *see* vocationalism
global 131
globalisation 93, 137
'graduate jobs' 15
graduates 124
Greenwich 47
'Groundhog Day' 37

Harbour, C. 14
Heath, A. 10
higher education (HE) 16, 18, 135
Higher Education Funding Council for England (HEFCE) 47
Higher Education Statistics Agency (HESA) 38
higher-level 14
higher-level apprenticeship *see* apprenticeships
Higher National Certificates (HNCs) 45
Higher National Diplomas (HNDs) 45
higher vocational pedagogy *see* vocationalism
Hodgson, A. 14
housing benefit 12

Index 143

Huddleston, P. 53
human capital theory 13
Hyland, T. 12

individualisation 94
immaterial labour 94
impression management 19
Individualised Learner Record (ILR) 38, 43, 47
informed-based training 134
Institute for Public Policy Research (IPPR) 12
intermediate level; *see* apprenticeships
international 131, 134, 139
'invisible learning' 125
Ipos MORI 46

Jameson, J. 1, 37, 131
job-specific knowledge 114
Jones, C. 12
judgements 125

Keynesian Welfarism 95
knowledge 79, 106, 107, 108, 109, 114, 117; applied knowledge 110, 114; knowledge-based economies 93; based learning 135; constructions of 5; disciplinary knowledge 81, 86, 101; domain-wide knowledge 83; essential knowledge 83; everyday knowledge 86; generic knowledge 83; job-specific knowledge 114; occupational knowledge 86, 135, 136; pedagogic 79, 81; 'personal practical knowledge' 80; 'powerful knowledge' 79, 101; practical knowledge 109, 113; practitioners/practice 118, 121; 'Putting Knowledge to Work' 5; (knowledge) society 138; subject knowledge 83; tacit knowledge 127; teachers' professional knowledge 80; teaching knowledge 84; theoretical 109, 112, 113, 114; theoretical frameworks 79; vertical knowledge 87; vocational knowledge 110; work-place knowledge 109
knowledgeable practitioners/practice; *see* knowledge
knowledge-based economies *see* knowledge
knowledge society *see* knowledge
Kress, G. 80

Lansley, A. 10
leadership 2, 23–6, 32, 34
league table 138
learner 79, 121
learning for life 137
'Learning from difficult experiences' 125
learning from peer review 84
'Learning through trial and error' 125
Leitch, S. 16
Lingfield Report 78
longitudinal progression routes 42, 48
Loo, S. 1, 78, 80, 86, 88, 131
loose coupling 24–5
Loughran, J. 80
lower achievers 115
lower-level 136
low-skills-based vocational provision 136
low-skilled labour market 136

McAfee, A. 10
McGettigan, A. 15
Mack, J. 10
macro 1
marketplace 22
maintenance grants/loans 9, 15
Major, J. 9
managerialism 25, 26
marketization 138
Marx, K. 10
mass customisation 94
massification 138
mentorship 126
mergers 22–34
meso 1
metaphor/metaphorical 23, 26, 27, 37, 86
micro 1
'middle child' 132
mixed vocational route *see* vocationalism
Modern Apprenticeships *see* apprenticeships
'muddling through' 126
multimodality 80

Naidoo, R. 16
National Apprenticeship Service (NAS) 12
National Audit Office 40
National Living Wage 12
National Minimum Wage 12

National Vocational Qualifications (NVQs) 12, 45, 131
nature of practice 117
Neo-Fordism 98
neo-liberalism 93
networked communities 138
newly qualified workers 121
new market state 19
new times 93
non-transferability 134
nursing 124

occupational: experiences 78, 84 (*see also* vocationalism); fields 135; identity 65, 67; knowledge (*see* knowledge); teaching 86
Office for Standards in Education (Ofsted) 11
'ongoing recontextualisation' *see* recontextualisation
open source 94
over-complexity 38

Palfreyman, D. 16, 18
paradoxes 41
Participation of Local Areas (POLAR) 47
partnerships 23, 27–8, 34
pathways; *see* apprenticeships
pedagogic 79, 81, 85, 138, 114, 120
pedagogic recontextualisation *see* recontextualisation
peer learning 122
peer-to-peer (P2P) 94
'perceptions of reality' 84
performative 127, 136
personal learning and thinking skills (PLTSs) 11
'personal practical knowledge' *see* knowledge
'playbor' 94
policy 22, 26, 30–1, 37
Pollard, A. 80
post-compulsory education sector 39, 134
post-Fordist 93, 138
post-qualification 118
'powerful knowledge' *see* knowledge
practical knowledge *see* knowledge
precariousness 94
Principals 24–35
private training organisations 13
Pro-ams 94

produsers 94
professional 45, 135
progression 38, 43, 45–8, 111, 112, 114
'Putting Knowledge to Work' *see* knowledge

qualifications 66, 71
quality 27–30, 69

Raikes, L. 13, 19
Raising of the Participation Age (RPA) 54
realistic learning environments 59
reclassificatory recontextualisation *see* recontextualisation
recontextualisation 79, 87, 110, 112, 119; content 79, 120; learners 120; 'ongoing recontextualisation' 87; pedagogic 79, 114, 120; reclassificatory 79; workplace 114, 120
reductive 136
reflective peer review 83, 84
relation between theory and practice 123
research 135
'reserve army of labour' 10, 137
restrictive and expansive learning centres and environments 100
restructuring 41
retail assistant 69
Review of Vocational Qualifications (Wolf Report) 55
Richard, D. 11, 12, 78
route into employment 131
Russell Group 42

Scott, P. 15, 16
'second-chance' 131
'sense-making' 38, 47
Shildrick, T. 11
Shulman, L. 79
Silver, R. 17
Simmons, R. 17
simple 48
skills 71; acquisition 134; employability 136
Skills Funding Agency (SFA) 11, 18
Smith, E. 65
Smithers, A. 12
social class inequalities 131
social construction of skill 73
social justice 100, 131
social mobility 10, 47, 131
social production 94, 99

Index

social relations 122
Sockice, D. 19
specialist centres 133
Spours, K. 14
status schism 136
stratification 137
structure 42
Student Loan Asset-Based Securities (SLABs) 15
students 10
subject knowledge *see* knowledge
supercomplex 37, 41, 47
sustainability 27–8

tacit dimension 86
tacit knowledge *see* knowledge
'Taking History' 84
Tapper, T. 16, 18
teachers/teaching 78, 80, 86; education curriculum 89; knowledge (*see* knowledge); professional knowledge (*see* knowledge); standards 83
Tech certificates 57
Tech levels 57
tertiary education (TE) 16
Thatcher, M. 10
theoretical knowledge *see* knowledge
trainees *see* apprenticeships
traineeships 65, 67, 69, 72, 74
trainee teachers 84
training of FE teachers 65, 78
training levy 9
'Training Packages' 67, 72
Train to Gain 9
'transfer' 127
transformation/transformative 34, 37
tripartite 138
typologists/typology 79, 131

'underclass' 11
undervalued skill 71
United Vocational Preparation 53
Universities and Colleges Admissions Service (UCAS) 43
University Technical Colleges (UTCs) 17
utilitarian 136

Verloop, N. 79
vertical knowledge *see* knowledge
vocational experiences *see* vocationalism
vocationalism: Australian vocational education and training system 4; dual vocational education and training system 134, 135, 139; education and training (VET) provision 37, 53, 65, 93, 131; English VET provision 139; 'English model' 1, 6; *see also* English model and 'English context'; experiences 78; General National Vocational Qualification (GNVQ) 53; general vocational education and qualifications 106, 107; higher vocational pedagogy 14, 18, 118; higher vocational programme 118; international VET systems 131; learning 61; low-skills-based vocational provision 136; mixed vocational route 133; pedagogy 5, 93; programmes 3, 58; qualifications 60, 108; school 133; training 78, 86; two VET models 135; vocational school (*see* vocationalism); voluntarist 132, 139

waged labour 101
wages 12, 134; *see* apprenticeships
Welfare to Work 9
widening participation 18
Willetts, D. 15, 16
Wolf, A. 11, 13, 14, 18, 55, 78
'women's work' 73
work-based learning 118
Work-Based Learning for Education Professionals Centre 80
work environment 117
work experience 62
work-place knowledge; *see* knowledge
workplace learning 79, 135
workplace recontextualisation *see* recontextualisation
workplace supervisors 124

Young, M. 79
Youth Training Scheme 9